MAKE SOME
BEER

MAKE SOME BEER

BEER

SMALL-BATCH RECIPES

from

BROOKLYN TO BAMBERG

ERICA SHEA & STEPHEN VALAND

Illustrations by Deryck Vonn Lee

CLARKSON POTTER/PUBLISHERS

NEW YORK

Published in the United States by Clarkson Potter/Publishers,
an imprint of the Crown Publishing Group, a division of
Random House LLC, a Penguin Random House Company,
New York.
www.crownpublishing.com
www.clarksonpotter.com

CLARKSON POTTER is a trademark and POTTER with colophon
is a registered trademark of Random House LLC.

Library of Congress Cataloging-in-Publication Data
Shea, Erica.
  Make some beer: small-batch recipes from Brooklyn to
Bamberg/Erica Shea and Stephen Valand; illustrations by
Deryck Vonn Lee.–1st ed.
     p. cm.
  Includes index.
1. Brewing–Amateurs' manuals. 2. Beer–Amateurs' manuals. 3.
Cooking (Beer)–Amateurs' manuals. 4. Cookbooks. I. Title.
  TP570 .S523 2014
  663'.42–dc23   2013034664

ISBN 978-0-804-13763-8
eBook ISBN 978-0-804-13764-5

Printed in the United States of America

Interior design: La Tricia Watford
Illustrations: Deryck Vonn Lee
Cover design: Jim Massey
Cover photograph: Marcos Mesa Sam Wordley/Shutterstock
Cover illustrations: (hops) Margocha8/Shutterstock;
(background) Palladin12/Shutterstock

10 9 8 7 6 5 4 3 2 1

First Edition

CONTENTS

SPRING 18

Berliner Weisse • Dandelion Gruit • Bière de Garde • Tapioca Ale • Chinook Single Hop IPA • Mulberry Wheat • Celery Salt Gose • Chamomile Blonde

PLUS: IPA Hummus • Pimento Beer Cheese • Beer Fruit Leather • Black Pepper, Parmesan, and Beer Grits • Spent Grain No-Rise Pizza Dough • Spent Grain Popovers • Spent Grain Peanut Butter Cookies

SUMMER 60

Ranger Creek's Mesquite Smoked Porter • Farmhouse Ale • Blended Fruit Beer • IPA, Belgian Style • Cucumber Saison • Table Beer • Strawberry Rhubarb Strong Ale • Oyster Singel

PLUS: Raw Oysters with Oyster Singel Mignonette • Farmhouse Ale Risotto • Moules à la Bière • Shandy Ice Pops

FALL 98

Bruxelles Blonde • Bruxelles Black • Fall Saison • Bacon Dubbel • Six Hop IPA • Sweet Potato Lager • Kriek • Hindy's Chocolate Stout • Ron Pattinson's Once Upon a Time: 1945 Mild

PLUS: Beer & Bacon Mac & Cheese • Abbey Onion Soup • Beer Beef Jerky

WINTER 138

Smoked Wheat • Peppercorn Rye • New Orleans Coffee Milk Stout • Rum Barrel Porter • Oatmeal Raisin Cookie Stout • Warrior Double IPA • Evil Twin's Christmas Eve at a New York City Hotel Room

PLUS: Bamberg Onion • Welsh Rarebit Beer Fondue • Beer-Soaked Oven Fries • Black Pepper Beer Poutine

INTRODUCTION

A question we get asked all the time is how we started Brooklyn Brew Shop—in interviews, by people passing through the market, by old classmates we haven't seen in years (and who don't recall Erica even liking beer). When you're introduced as someone who created a beer company, people are curious and want to know how you did it. And the "how" they expect involves us being industrial designers, or having MBA degrees, or growing up surrounded by beer. They imagine business proposals and investor meetings or rich relatives who indulged us. They don't expect our answer to start with, "Well, we quit our jobs and went backpacking in Europe for seven weeks."

BUT THAT'S HOW IT ALL STARTED.

The idea for Brooklyn Brew Shop existed before our trip. It existed from the first time we tried to make beer and realized there wasn't a single place in New York City to gather supplies. It existed every Saturday we spent brewing around Stephen's roommates with our often-improvised equipment. It existed in every bottle we shared with the explanation that "yes, we made this." Brooklyn Brew Shop existed for the two of us in the conversations we would have for a solid year about how to do it right, how to make brewing feel more like cooking, and how to make it affordable, approachable, and exciting. We became obsessed with re-creating the sheer delight we experienced from making beer with everyone.

Brooklyn Brew Shop existed as something we could do, as something we really should do, and as something we really wanted to do. But the question that kept coming up was whether this was something we were actually ready to do. Or more to the point: Was this something we were ready to do together?

So we bought the domain brooklynbrewshop .com and started planning a backpacking trip. The seven weeks we would spend backpacking through Europe would serve two purposes. The first would be to sample a lot of beer by drinking our way through historic regions and styles. We'd visit breweries and absorb a wealth of brewing knowledge by, well, absorbing a wealth of beer.

The second was a test. Were we ready to spend every moment of every day together? Would we still be kind to each other when tired and hun-

gry and strained from lifting heavy things (like a 35-pound backpack)? Was our relationship ready for a business and our imagined business ready for a very real relationship? We were young (Stephen 23, Erica 25). Our relationship was younger. And even though we were obsessed with brewing, our beer education was youngest of all.

So we planned, and we saved. Erica researched each stop, obsessively tracking and retracking the best means of transportation. Stephen pored over profiles on couchsurfing.org, a site where people offer travelers a free place to stay, to find the best matches based on profile pictures, music choices, number of cats, and whether or not they loved food and cooking.

In the time leading up to the trip, our conversations alternated between the beers we wanted to brew, how to start Brooklyn Brew Shop, and the weird or useful facts we were learning about Oslo or Brussels or Amsterdam. We were nervous and excited. We sent emails to potential suppliers and brewed test batches for the first few beers we were planning to release, but the opening dates of the Brooklyn Flea (the artisan market where we hoped to launch Brooklyn Brew Shop) were still just marks on our calendar. We booked flights, gave notice at our jobs, visited the doctor while we still had health insurance, and sublet our apartments—all the while brewing up batch after batch. We threw a going-away party, drank most of the beer we had brewed, and on April 6, 2009, left knowing that whatever happened over the next seven weeks, the lives we returned to would be different. And we were ready.

Our trip started in Oslo. Stephen's grandparents and great-grandparents immigrated to Brooklyn from Norway, but he'd never left North America until this trip. We knew climate-wise it would have been better to end there in May rather than start there in early April, but we could adjust to climate. The cost of good beer, however, was a little hard to swallow. We met our first host, Sara; went to our first bar, Grünerløkka Brygghus; ordered our first beer; shelled out 89 kroner (about $15) for a pint; and drank up.

Remnants of snow, blustery breezes, and pricey pints were soon the least of our problems. Easter was just a few days away, and, it turned out, Scandinavians take that holiday pretty seriously. Watching chains being locked over the doors of the beer fridge the Wednesday before Easter was a puzzling sight to say the least. The city shut down, and our beer tour went dry for a couple of days.

From Oslo we took a Neil Diamond–blaring overnight "cruise" to Copenhagen, Denmark, where we were staying with a Finnish girl who lost her voice and, along with it, any Danish she had picked up since immigrating. She took us to a bodega where we drank 25-cent beers. Bodegas in Copenhagen aren't places to pick up household necessities in the middle of the night like in New York. They're more like VFW halls. Wood-paneled and full of old men. Plowing through a pack of cigarettes that couldn't have been helping her voice, she rasped through a cloud of smoke that young people didn't really come here but that beer was impossibly cheap, and it was the only kind of bar where you could still smoke cigarettes.

For the brief window during Easter weekend when bars would be open, our Finnish friend also took us to an amazing subterranean spot, Lord Nelson Bar, the craft beer bar where she worked, followed by another and another. We rented used and mostly rickety bikes, ate smørrebrød from Aamanns, and became enamored by Danish craft beer culture. Never having the same beer twice and finding tap handles labeled with handscrawled strips of paper and tape is the ultimate way to discover the beers of a city. No matter how much we learned (and by that we mean drank), it became pretty obvious how much more we had to go.

Time flies when you're riding bikes, so even though we were both ready to plant our flags and live, breathe, and drink everything Danish, we knew this was just the beginning. Copenhagen went on our list of places we would need to come back to someday.

Our next stop was Berlin. When you think of beer and Germany, you probably think Munich, Bamberg, or Cologne—not Berlin. We knew that there really weren't any breweries there and that a Berliner weisse (see page 22), the tart wheat beer named after the city, was going to be hard to find. But it was to Berlin—David Bowie, weird art, New York before Giuliani but without crime—that we had to go. We were staying with a couple who hosted underground Finnish supper clubs monthly in an unused building, and took self-portrait photographs wearing fur hats and stoic expressions. They had as many records as we did (Erica grew up in a record shop) and DJ'd '60s garage rock on weekends.

On borrowed bikes, we stocked up at the Turkish market, ate arguably the best falafel in the Western world at Mo's, made dinner for our hosts, and told them about the beer company we planned on starting. We stumbled upon a brewpub called Hops & Barley in Friedrichshain, drank *märzens* in a park, biked endlessly, and washed down the impossibly crisp fried chicken at Henne with giant mugs of malty Bavarian lager.

Our beer tour had changed; it was no longer about absorbing the historical styles of a place. It was simply about absorbing a place and beer's place in it.

So when we got to the Czech Republic, we skipped the Staropramen Brewery just outside Prague and spent an entire day drinking Velko-popovický Kozel at U Černého Vola (At the Black Ox) while eating pickled cheese and trying our best to say, "světlé pivo" (light beer) and "černé pivo" (dark beer), which our host Matthias spelled out phonetically. In the shadow of Prague Castle, the bar was created for locals. The tourists who flocked to the area were not particularly welcome, or at least weren't sought after. We were required to order for ourselves in Czech. We said "děkuji" (thank you), and the bartender said "goodbye." We said goodbye to Matthias—or rather, see you soon (as he would be staying with Stephen when he traveled to New York for the summer).

In Hungary, we washed down rancid goose cracklings with a quite adept lager at a brewpub in Budapest. We drank jug wine and ate sausage, both obtained at the Dolac market in Zagreb, and caught up with a college friend attending med school there.

We arrived in Venice at five a.m., exhausted and sore after taking an overnight train for which we accidentally booked seats instead of a sleeping car. Hauling our packs, we roamed the city from square to square, completely lost with no one on the streets but fishmongers at the Mercato di Rialto, unpacking the freshest seafood we'd ever seen. At this point, we had no euros. Due to suspected international bank fraud, all our cards had been deactivated when Stephen tried withdrawing $20,000 in Hungary after a bad conversion into forints. A bird then shit on Erica's head. We laughed, cleaned it up as best we could, roamed until we found Wi-Fi so we could orient ourselves, and realized that we were utterly in love—with a city, with our trip, with each other, and with the future endeavor we were going to start together. And we still had four weeks to go.

We ate *cichetti* in Venice, *aperitivi* in Florence, and *porchetta* in Rome, then took an overnight boat to Barcelona, where we ate tapas and ordered glass after glass of cerveza after realizing we had once again landed in a city on a national holiday (this time May Day). Morning plans to visit the Picasso museum would have to wait a day.

Paris was our next stop. We stayed with one of Erica's former track-and-field teammates, Andrea (a German pole-vaulter an inch shorter than Stephen and much taller than Erica), and her Chilean boyfriend. We wandered an incredibly vast city as best we could, stumbling upon a bar where no one spoke English. Stephen mustered up the best phrases he could remember from middle-school French class, and Erica said, "Je suis une pomme de terre" because it was the only thing she knew. Beer has a knack for breaking down language barriers. The bartender found a dusty, unintentionally cellar-aged, 12% alcohol Belgian ale and poured it into two matching chalices he pulled from a case behind the bar that seemed to just be waiting for our arrival. Down the block, men were playing Paul Simon covers and calling it jazz. After waking up the next day to find a potato peeler in Stephen's shirt pocket, we left France.

If any place in the world could be called beer mecca, it would be Belgium, and despite accidentally staying in Brussels's red light district, our brief visit was still quite heavenly. Visiting breweries like Cantillon that were older than our grandparents, we casually drank beer from the corner store that we would have reserved for special occasions back in the States. Belgium strengthened our understanding of the craft behind beer and the heritage that can go into every glass. All of a sudden our kitchen stove was part of a much larger tradition than we ever realized, and we were ready to join it together.

We swung through Amsterdam and back to Paris after hearing that the last film Stephen had worked on was accepted to premiere at Cannes. We rented a car and drove through Burgundy down to the south of France. We slept in the car. Stephen learned to drive stick through towns that were otherworldly charming by day and seemingly haunted or vampire-ridden by night.

We began talking less and less about what we would see next and more and more about Brooklyn Brew Shop and what we would brew once we got back.

We flew to London, exhausted, and stayed with a bartender in Hackney who was super into the real ale campaign, started in the 1970s with the intention to get the English drinking fresh, locally sourced, traditional ales. That campaign is also part of the reason why people joke that English beers are warm and uncarbonated. While this is somewhat true, the Brits do a really good job with them. So we drank ale after ale from cask after cask. We compared their Indian spice stores with ours and added to the list of beers we wanted to brew upon our return.

Our tour finished in Dublin, where we drank oyster stouts and red ales at Porter House and scribbled grand plans in tattered travel journals.

But our beer-making trip didn't end there.

We got back on May 21, 2009, emailed the Brooklyn Flea, put in orders with our new vendors, tried hand-sawing plastic tubes and drilling holes in rubber stoppers from scientific and medical suppliers because the parts we needed didn't yet exist, and brewed a Belgian-style tripel that we bottled with orange-blossom honey.

Forty-five days later (just two days longer than our trip), we launched Brooklyn Brew Shop.

Back in Brooklyn we obsessed over every new beer we came across. Craft beer in the United States kept getting more interesting. Not bound by any one set of laws or traditions, American brewers could pick and choose their influences—German malts with American hops, Belgian yeasts with South Asian spices. Much like the batches we developed on our stovetops, the best of these American breweries combined tradition with new ingredients and techniques.

These are the breweries we took every opportunity we could to visit. Day trips by train turned into weekends in nearby Philadelphia, Boston, and DC so we could talk to brewers. We tacked days onto friends' cross-country weddings to seek out the smallest and most interesting breweries, which often didn't export beer out of their states—never mind to Brooklyn.

We hauled beer back for the people who volunteered with us that first holiday season—and then for our employees. We would sit down for "two o'clock tastings" where we'd bring in every beer we could from a particular brewery and take notes on everything from appearance and aroma to the overall taste of each beer.

We started recording our interviews with the breweries we visited, taking short videos to remember them by. We swapped care packages with the brewers afterward, sending them our favorite Brooklyn items: McClure's spicy pickles and Liddabit Sweets beer and pretzel caramels. We learned new techniques and adapted some of them to re-create certain styles or beer characteristics at home. We were inspired. Beer became our life, and our life as we know it today started with that amazing trip, which began out of a desire to share with the world something we loved—but ended with the world sharing much more than we had anticipated.

That's how every trip ends now—with a greater understanding of beer, of the places we've been and still dream of going, and a return to Brooklyn, our cat, Cat, and our dog, Porter, and brewing on our stovetop. These are the recipes inspired by our travels, the tips we've learned from brewing masters, and the regional ingredients we were introduced to along the way. We hope that these recipes will inspire not only your next batch, but your next brew trip.

HAPPY BREWING!
ERICA & STEPHEN

HOW-TO-BREW REFRESHER

If you've used our Beer Making Kit in the past or have a few batches of beer under your belt, feel free to skip right to the recipes (page 22). But if your equipment has collected some dust since its last brew day or you simply feel the need to brush up, we've put together a quick guide to the basics of brewing.

We recommend first-timers start off with some of this book's more straightforward recipes like Bruxelles Blonde (page 102), Chinook Single Hop IPA (page 38), or Farmhouse Ale (page 68), while experienced brewers may want to check out some of the more adventurous beers such as the Kriek (page 124), Celery Salt Gose (page 46), or Bacon Dubbel (page 112). And if you're looking for additional recipes or more in-depth brewing information, check out our first book, *Brooklyn Brew Shop's Beer Making Book: 52 Seasonal Recipes for Small Batches*.

ONE THE MASH

For this step you are pretty much making a pot of oatmeal. In a stockpot, heat the water on high. When the temperature reaches 160°F, add all the grain to mash in. Then stir and check the temperature regularly to make sure it stays between 144°F (62°C) and 152°F (67°C). After 60 minutes, raise the heat to 170°F while stirring constantly to mash out.

TWO THE SPARGE

Place a fine-mesh strainer over a stockpot large enough to hold at least 1.5 gallons (5.68 liters). Pour the mash into the strainer, reserving the collected liquid in the pot. Pour the sparging water over the grain gently and evenly. Recirculate the liquid through the grains two or three times to extract all the fermentable sugars. Reserve the grain (now known as spent grain) for future recipes (see Spent-Grain Primer, page 56).

VARIATION FOR FIVE GALLONS

Line a 6.5-gallon (24.6-liter) plastic bottling bucket with a sparging bag. Pour the mash into the bag, straining the liquid into the bucket. Pour the sparging water over the grain gently and evenly. Recirculate the liquid through the grains two or three times to extract all the fermentable sugars. Reserve the grain (now known as spent grain) for future recipes (see page 56).

THREE THE BOIL

Bring the liquid (now known as wort) to a boil. Reduce the heat to a slow boil and start a timer for 60 to 90 minutes, depending on the recipe. Add applicable hops, fruits, and spices at the times listed in the specific recipe.

FOUR FERMENTATION

Prepare an ice bath in your sink. After the boil is complete, put the pot in the ice bath to cool the wort to 70°F (21°C). Use a funnel to pour the cooled wort into a sanitized fermenter. Top off the fermenter (to the 1- or 5-gallon mark) with cold water if levels are low. Pitch the yeast and shake the fermenter to oxygenate your wort. Attach a blow-off tube for the first 3 days, then switch to an airlock when vigorous fermenting has subsided.

Store the fermenter somewhere dark and cool— for ales between 65°F (18°C) and 75°F (24°C).

FIVE BOTTLING

When the surface of your beer is clear (usually after 2 weeks of fermentation), your beer is ready to be bottled. Sanitize bottles, caps, pots, and siphoning equipment.

You'll have to siphon your beer twice when it's time to bottle. First, from your fermenter into a stockpot with a little sugar and water. The type of sugar changes depending on the beer you're making, so check the individual recipe for more info. The second time you siphon is from the stockpot into finished bottles.

To siphon, you'll need a stockpot large enough to hold the amount of beer you're bottling, a bowl filled with a solution of equal parts water and sanitizer, soft rubber tubing, a tubing clamp, and a racking cane, which is a hard plastic tube with a curve at the top. First, slide the open tubing clamp over the soft rubber tubing about 5 inches. Coil the soft rubber tubing and submerge it in the sanitizer solution so that it fills up with liquid and pushes out any air bubbles. Pinch the tubing clamp shut. Attach the end of the soft rubber tubing opposite the tubing clamp to the curved end of the racking cane while being careful not to lose any of the sanitizer solution.

Remove the stopper from the fermenter, and submerge the racking cane until its tip rests just above the sediment along the bottom of the beer. Lower the opposite end of the soft rubber tubing into the sink, and open the tubing clamp. Allow the sanitizer to flow out. Close tubing clamp as soon as beer begins to flow out from the soft rubber tubing. Move the end of the soft rubber tubing from the sink into a pot and open the tubing clamp, allowing the beer to fill the stockpot and the beer to blend evenly with the sugar solution already in the stockpot.

Gravity is your best friend when siphoning, so make sure your fermenter is higher than whatever you're filling. Siphon again into bottles with self-sealing swing-top closures or non-twist-off-top beer bottles that you can seal with a bottle capper and caps. Store your bottles in a dark place for 2 weeks.

SIX DRINKING

For most recipes, your beer will be ready to open 2 weeks after bottling. Chill and enjoy.

BREWING EQUIPMENT

(SEE SOURCES, PAGE 173, FOR INFO ON WHERE TO BUY)

STOCKPOTS For one gallon of beer, a couple of pots that hold six to eight quarts each work well. For five gallons, use two large stockpots (or one giant one). You'll need to be able to boil 6.5 gallons at a time.

FINE-MESH STRAINER For a one-gallon batch, we use a sturdy, stainless-steel ten-inch mesh strainer to hold all the grain at once. For five gallons, a nylon mesh sparging bag and a 6.5-gallon plastic bucket with a spigot are necessary to strain all the grain.

FUNNEL We use an eight-inch funnel with a mesh screen attachment to catch hop residue.

THERMOMETER You'll need a thermometer that can register temperatures as low as 70°F (21°C) and as high as 200°F (93°C) and is long enough to take readings from multiple locations in your pot. We use a dual-scale 12-inch (30-centimeter) lab thermometer.

HYDROMETER This measures the density of liquids. You take one reading before adding the yeast (original gravity) and one reading when you think fermentation is done (final gravity). If the ABV (alcohol by volume) falls short of what is listed in the recipe, let the beer keep fermenting.

SANITIZER A good food-grade no-rinse sanitizer will make sure that the yeast you're brewing with is the only microorganism fermenting your beer. We make one. Starsan and One-Step are great, too. Follow the manufacturer's instructions on how to properly dilute it. We always have a sanitizer-filled spray bottle on hand to resanitize surfaces throughout the brew day.

FERMENTER For one gallon, use a one-gallon glass jug. For five-gallon batches, a glass carboy is our preferred fermenter. Plastic fermenters are okay in the short term, but can get scratched easily and harbor bacteria. We definitely recommend investing in glass or stainless steel.

STOPPER For our one-gallon batches we use a screw-cap stopper with a hole that fits both the tubing and an airlock. For 5 gallons, use a rubber stopper with a hole drilled through it or a molded plastic carboy bung.

AIRLOCK Essential for fermentation, this allows gases to escape without letting anything foreign into your beer. We find the three-piece chambered variety the easiest to clean.

RACKING CANE OR AUTO-SIPHON When your beer is done fermenting it needs to be siphoned out of the fermenter. Either a racking cane or an auto-siphon will work fine.

SOFT TUBING Three and a half to four feet of $5/16$-inch diameter clear plastic food-grade tubing is necessary for siphoning and acting as a blow-off tube for a one-gallon batch. For a five-gallon batch, you'll also need a three-foot length of one-inch diameter vinyl food-grade tubing for a blow-off tube to fit the larger opening of a five-gallon carboy.

TUBING CLAMP This allows you to easily stop and start the flow of beer when filling bottles.

BOTTLE CAPPER The basic double-lever versions work great.

BOTTLE CAPS Crown caps, to use with the capper.

BOTTLES You can reuse most non-twist-off beer bottles with a standard double-lever bottle capper. Craft beer bottles are great.

BELGIAN-STYLE BOTTLES When bottling beers that require wild yeasts or increased aging periods, we recommend using Belgian-style swing-top bottles, which can withstand greater degrees of pressure than your typical beer bottle.

SPECIALTY KITCHEN
EQUIPMENT

DIGITAL SCALE Very useful for measuring grain and hops. For weighing grain, you'll want accuracy down to a tenth of a pound. Hops are much smaller, so they require accuracy to a tenth of an ounce.

DEHYDRATOR By no means necessary, but if you are regularly drying out your spent grains to mill into flour (see page 56), it is a great piece of equipment to have. And it makes the Beer Fruit Leather (page 54) a snap.

SMOKER If you have one, by all means use it for smoking grain (see Mesquite Smoked Porter, page 64).

BREWING INGREDIENTS

Much like the recipes in this book were inspired by our travels, the grain, hops, yeast, and specialty ingredients we use for these recipes are often those from that region. Here is a breakdown of the brewing ingredients in this book (and a few substitutions if necessary). See Sources (page 173) for info on where to buy ingredients.

GRAIN

Without grain, there couldn't be beer. Grain, typically malted barley, gives beer its sweetness, body, frothy head, and fermentable sugars (very important for making alcohol). All malted barley must be milled prior to use. Milling cracks open the grain's hearty husk so that its full malt character can be carried through to the finished beer. Malted barley is kilned in various ways resulting in a wide range of flavors ranging from a light candy sweetness to warm baking bread to burnt raisin toffee. Below is a list of some of our favorite and most essential grains.

BASE MALTS American 2-row, English Pale, English Mild, Maris Otter, German Pilsner, Munich, Vienna, Belgian Pilsner, French Pale (Belgian Pilsner can be substituted in the Bière de Garde, page 30, if French Pale is not available.)

CARAMEL MALTS Caramel (or Crystal) 10–120, Cara-Pils, Special-B, Caramel Amber

TOASTED MALTS Aromatic, Biscuit, Victory (works as a good substitute for Biscuit)

(continues)

ROASTED MALTS Roasted Barley, Black, Chocolate

SMOKED Beechwood, Mesquite (see Mesquite Smoked Porter, page 64)

NON-BARLEY Pale Wheat, White Wheat, Torrified Wheat, Rye, Flaked Oats, Tapioca

HOPS

Hops are a crop and depending on the season (or popularity), certain hops (such as Amarillo and Simcoe) can be hard to come by. Use an alternative hop that has the same bitterness level and similar tasting notes for the best results (see table, opposite).

YEAST

While a brewer's job when brewing is turning grain into sugar, converting that sugar into alcohol is the work of yeast. It can, of course, be a little creepy knowing that billions of cells of yeast go into every batch of beer you make, but their impact on your finished beer cannot go unrecognized. Flavors both good and bad come from different strains of yeast that have evolved over generations in breweries around the world. Banana, clove, green apple, butterscotch, plastic, adhesives, and rubbing alcohol are all potential aromas that can arise from yeast during fermentation.

NOTE: While we package our yeast in one-gallon size, most commercial yeast packets are designed for five-gallon batches—just use a third of the packet.

THREE TYPES OF YEAST FOR MANY TYPES OF BEER

ALE YEAST

Comfortable at room temperatures, ale yeast reproduces rapidly and settles to the bottom over the course of two weeks, forming a layer of sediment called "trub." Ale yeast can be found in a bunch of styles ranging from IPAs to stouts, porters, red ales, saisons, to most other styles where a fuller, often fruitier, yeast profile is acceptable.

LAGER YEAST

On the other hand, lager yeast is mainly responsible for, you guessed it, lagers. Derived from the Old German word for storage, a lager typically requires months at lower temperatures (around 54°F/12°C) to fully ferment and mature. The yeast sits at the bottom of the beer for the entire fermentation, which helps you get a clearer beer in the end.

WILD YEAST

Brettanomyces (or brett for short) is the double-edged sword of fermentation. It's wild, which means it's in the air all around us. Brett can help contribute to a sour beer, which can be an acquired taste for even a well-seasoned beer fan. Preventing wild yeast from taking over your beer is the reason you need to sanitize whatever comes in contact with your beer on brew day. If used intentionally, you may be looking at a waiting period of months to well over a year for a complex, sip-worthy glass of sour beer. If unintentional, you may say your beer is infected. Check out the Kriek recipe (page 124) for a taste of what wild yeast can do to a beer.

GUIDE TO HOPS

HOPS	COUNTRY	BITTERNESS	DESCRIPTION
AMARILLO	U.S.	Medium to High	Grapefruit/Tart/Lively
CASCADE	U.S.	Medium	Floral/Citrus/Pine
CENTENNIAL	U.S.	High	Rounded/Pine Needle/Tangerine
CHALLENGER	U.K.	Medium	Spicy/Moss/Red Apple
CHINOOK	U.S.	High	Pine/Black Pepper/Grapefruit
CITRA	U.S.	High	Passion Fruit/Lime/Mango
CLUSTER	U.S.	Medium	Spicy/Floral/Earthy
EAST KENT GOLDING	U.K.	Low to Medium	Dried Flowers/Moss/Plum
FUGGLE	U.K.	Low	Dried Maple Wood/Wet Dirt/Old Man
GALAXY	Australia	High	Peach/Passion Fruit/Tropical
GLACIER	U.S.	Medium	Lemon Iced Tea/Licorice/Apricot
HALLERTAU	Germany	Low	New Leaves/Crisp/Grassy
MAGNUM	U.S./Germany	High	Clean/Crisp/Bitter
NORTHERN BREWER	U.S./Germany/U.K.	Medium	Damp Forest/Mint/Pear
PACIFIC JADE	New Zealand	High	Herbal/Fresh Citrus/Black Pepper
PACIFICA	New Zealand	Low to Medium	Fruity/Juicy/Marmalade
PROGRESS	U.K.	Medium	Sweet Dirt/Berry/Juniper
SAAZ	Czech	Low	Dried Herbs/White Pepper/Apples
SIMCOE	U.S.	High	Fresh Pine Needles/Passion Fruit/Black Pepper
SORACHI ACE	Japan/U.S.	High	Lemon Herbal Tea/White Floral/Dusty
SPALTZ	Germany	Low	Crisp/Fresh/Ferns
STRISSELSPALT	France	Low	Mild/Light Floral/Straw
STYRIAN GOLDING	Slovenia	Low to Medium	White Pepper/Moss/Undergrowth
TETTNANG	Germany	Low	White Flowers/Straw/Peach
WARRIOR	U.S.	High	Clean/Lemon/Ice
WILLAMETTE	U.S.	Low	Herbal/Woody/Pleasant

SPRING

TO US

is all about

BALANCING

• ★ • ///////////////// • ★ •

the long, bright days of summer to come with the still-present crispness left over from winter. From The Bruery's tart take on the classic Berliner Weisse to Jenlain's traditional French Bière de Garde and Upright Brewing's modern twist on the hopless gruit, our spring beers strike that same balance.

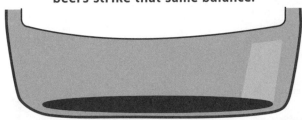

THE BREWERIES

THAT INSPIRED OUR BREWS

THE BRUERY
(ORANGE COUNTY, CA)
BERLINER WEISSE

THE KERNEL
(LONDON, ENGLAND)
CHINOOK SINGLE HOP IPA

UPRIGHT BREWING
(PORTLAND, OR)
DANDELION GRUIT

CARTON BREWING
(ATLANTIC HIGHLANDS, NJ)
MULBERRY WHEAT

JENLAIN
(JENLAIN, FRANCE)
BIÈRE DE GARDE

GASTHAUS & GOSEBRAUEREI BAYERISCHER BAHNHOF
(LEIPZIG, GERMANY)
CELERY SALT GOSE

PAUSA CAFE
(SALUZZO, ITALY)
TAPIOCA ALE

HILL FARMSTEAD
(GREENSBORO BEND, VT)
CHAMOMILE BLONDE

PLUS: IPA HUMMUS • PIMENTO BEER CHEESE • BEER FRUIT LEATHER • BLACK PEPPER, PARMESAN, AND BEER GRITS • SPENT GRAIN PRIMER & RECIPES

THE BRUERY

ORANGE COUNTY, CA

The occasional dodging of fast-moving forklifts and necessary leaping over shallow pools of water and sanitizer while assistant brewers lift, fill, and clean kegs can sometimes make a brewery tour feel more like a factory inspection. That's even before being outfitted with a pair of safety glasses where required.

Moments in breweries like these, strolling past stacked pallets far from the tasting room, often have us yearning for the kitchen where we can focus, not on the mechanics and logistics of beer delivery, but on the flavors and techniques of just making beer. When brewing is a job, it's easy to think of beer as business instead of food.

We like drinking beer much more than we like spreadsheets, and so does the staff of The Bruery, where a wall of beer aging in barrels towers over a fifteen-barrel brewhouse crammed inside a building located near the back of a random SoCal industrial park.

On the day of our visit The Bruery announced that it will cease production of Orchard White—their flagship, easy-drinking witbier.

Brewers who put business first don't typically get rid of their top-selling beer. "We either could fetch a lot of funding and build a much bigger brewery, and do a lot more draft beer and a lot more Orchard White and

approachable beers," says The Bruery's Ben Weiss. "Or we do what we always wanted to do, which is fill a ton of oak barrels with sour beers, strong ales, and really experimental things."

The Bruery doesn't make any easy beers. Everything it brews is complex—both to drink and to produce. Enjoying Bruery beers reminds us why we started brewing in the first place and inspires us to make beers that, in the end, just make us happy.

> "OR WE DO WHAT WE ALWAYS WANTED TO DO, WHICH IS FILL A TON OF OAK BARRELS WITH SOUR BEERS, STRONG ALES, AND REALLY EXPERIMENTAL THINGS."
>
> —BEN WEISS,
> *DIRECTOR OF MARKETING*

BERLINER WEISSE

5.5% ABV

PREP

1 cup (0.24 l) water

0.2 lb (90.72 g) German Pilsner malt for sour mash

60-MINUTE MASH AT 152°F (67°C)

2 qt (1.89 l) water, plus 1 gal (3.79 l) for sparging

1 lb (453.59 g) German Pilsner malt

1 lb (453.59 g) Pale Wheat malt

0.2 lb (90.72 g) acidulated malt

*All grains should be milled (see page 15).

60-MINUTE BOIL

0.2 oz (5.67 g) Tettnang hops

FERMENT

Wheat ale yeast, such as Safbrew WB-06 (see note, page 16)

3 Tbsp (63 g) honey, for bottling

WE LOVE THE LACTIC TARTNESS THAT A SOUR MASH GIVES THIS BEER. AND WHILE WE DRINK IT STRAIGHT AS A REFRESHING PALATE CLEANSER, TRADITIONALLY IT WAS SERVED WITH A SHOT OF RASPBERRY OR WOODRUFF SYRUP TO CUT THE TARTNESS. NAPOLEON FAMOUSLY CALLED IT "THE CHAMPAGNE OF THE NORTH."

PREP Three days before brewing, heat 1 cup (0.24 liter) water in a small pot over high heat to 130°F (54°C). Turn off the heat, add the 0.2 pound (90.72 grams) German Pilsner malt, and stir gently. The temperature should reduce to 120°F (49°C) within 1 minute. Cover the pot and steep the grains for 45 minutes at 120°F (49°C). Every 10 minutes, stir and take the temperature. If the grain gets too cold, turn the heat to high and stir until the temperature rises to 120°F (49°C). After 45 minutes, cover the surface of the grains with plastic wrap so no air touches the grains, and leave for 3 days in a spot that reaches 115°F (46°C), such as over a radiator or space heater or in a gas oven with only the pilot light on. This is how to make a "sour mash."

MASH In a medium stockpot, heat 2 quarts (1.89 liters) water over high heat to 160°F (70°C). Add all the malts and stir gently. The temperature should reduce to 150°F (66°C) within 1 minute. Turn off the heat. Steep the grains for 60 minutes between 144°F and 152°F

(62°C and 67°C). Every 10 minutes, stir and take the temperature. If the grains get too cold, turn the heat to high and stir until the temperature rises to that range, then turn off the heat. With 10 minutes left, in a second medium stockpot heat 1 gallon (3.79 liters) water to 170°F (77°C). After the grains have steeped for 60 minutes, turn the heat to high and stir until the temperature reaches 170°F (77°C). Turn off the heat.

SPARGE Place a fine-mesh strainer over a stockpot and pour the grains (including those from the sour mash) into the strainer, reserving the liquid. Pour the 1 gallon (3.79 liters) of 170°F (77°C) water over the grains. Recirculate the collected liquid through the grains once.

BOIL Return the pot with the liquid to the stove and bring to a boil over high heat. When the liquid starts to foam, reduce the heat to a slow boil. Add the Tettnang hops after 20 minutes. After 50 minutes, prepare an ice bath by stopping the sink and filling it halfway with water and ice. At the 60-minute mark, turn off the heat. Place the pot in the ice bath and cool to 70°F (21°C), about 30 minutes.

FERMENT Using a funnel and a strainer, pour the liquid into a sanitized fermenter. Add water as needed to fill the jug to the 1-gallon mark. Add the yeast, sanitize your hands, cover the mouth of the jug with one hand, and shake to distribute evenly. Attach a sanitized stopper and tubing to the fermenter and insert the other end of the tubing into a small bowl of sanitizing solution. The solution will begin to bubble as the yeast activates, pushing gas through the tube. Wait 2 to 3 days, until the bubbling has slowed, then replace the tubing system with an airlock. Wait 11 more days, then bottle, using the honey (see page 13 for bottling instructions).

//

SUGGESTED FOOD PAIRINGS Goat cheese, watermelon salad, poppyseed cake

FOR 5 GALLONS

PREP 5 cups (1.18 liters) water; 1 pound (453.59 grams) German Pilsner malt for sour mash

60-MINUTE MASH AT 152°F (67°C)
2½ gallons (9.46 liters) water, plus 5 gallons (18.93 liters) for sparging; 5 pounds (2267.96 grams) German Pilsner malt; 5 pounds (2267.96 grams) White Wheat malt; 1 pound (453.59 grams) acidulated malt

60-MINUTE BOIL 1 ounce (28.35 grams) Tettnang hops

FERMENT Wheat ale yeast, such as Safbrew WB-06; 1 cup (340 grams) honey, for bottling

UPRIGHT BREWING

PORTLAND, OR

BREWERY

If it hasn't become clear by now, we like brewing on the small scale. It frees us up to use interesting ingredients and methods when making a batch of beer. Economy of scale becomes just another phrase in the MBA book collecting dust on our bookshelf. We often say that brewing on a small scale means you can make beer in the comfort of your own kitchen—no longer does your favorite hobby need to be relegated to the garage or basement.

But what if you really like your basement? Forget the semifinished bachelor-pad-with-a-dartboard basement. What if your basement were actually a charming little brewery pumping out some of the most interesting beers in a city saturated in craft beer?

When it comes to eating and drinking, Portland is a city devoted to good taste that defies boundaries of both geography and time. More than 40 percent of all draft beer sold in Oregon is of the craft variety. As of 2013, the city of Portland has 49 breweries. If you look past the shimmer of stainless steel when visiting Upright Brewing, you'll notice more similarities to a nineteenth-century brewhouse tended by monks than to your average big brewery. You certainly won't find lemongrass, hyssop, bitter orange peel, or Szechwan peppercorns in an average brewery, let alone all in one beer as you do in Upright's Reggae Junkie Gruit.

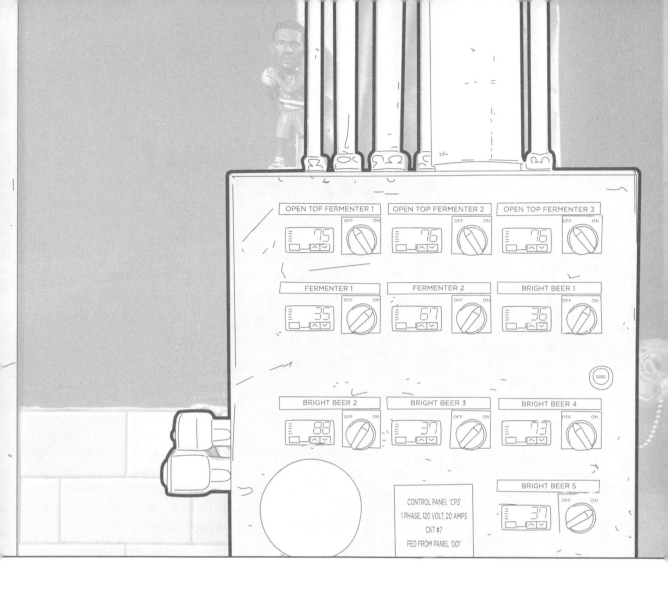

Beer, as a general rule, is made of malted barley, water, yeast, and hops. Gruit is a traditional style that excludes the hops, which provide bitterness, big aromas, and overall balance to a beer. A beer made without hops needs ingredients like those in Upright's gruit to provide all those things. So when brewing a gruit, a good spice store becomes a vital resource.

WANT MORE GRUIT? TRY PROFESSOR FRITZ BRIEM'S 13TH-CENTURY GRUT BEER.

DANDELION GRUIT

4.7% ABV

60-MINUTE MASH AT 152°F (67°C)

2 qt (1.89 l) water, plus 1 gal (3.79 l) for sparging

1.6 lb (725.75 g) Belgian Pilsner malt

0.25 lb (113.40 g) White Wheat malt

*All grains should be milled (see page 15).

60-MINUTE BOIL

7 dandelion leaves

1 Tbsp (10 g) whole black peppercorns

Peel from 1 lemon

FERMENT

Belgian ale yeast, such as Safbrew T-58 (see note, page 16)

3 Tbsp (63 g) honey, for bottling

FOR OUR TAKE ON A GRUIT, WE USE DANDELION GREENS, BLACK PEPPERCORNS, WHITE WHEAT, AND LEMON PEEL FOR A HOPLESS BEER THAT'S A LITTLE SPICY, LIGHTLY BITTER, AND HERBACEOUS WITH A DELICATE FLORAL AROMA. AND WHILE IT MAY LACK HOPS, IT CERTAINLY DOES NOT LACK FLAVOR.

MASH In a medium stockpot, heat 2 quarts (1.89 liters) water over high heat to 160°F (70°C). Add all the malts and stir gently. The temperature should reduce to 150°F (66°C) within 1 minute. Turn off the heat. Steep the grains for 60 minutes between 144°F and 152°F (62°C and 67°C). Every 10 minutes, stir and take the temperature. If the grains get too cold, turn the heat to high and stir until the temperature rises to that range, then turn off the heat. With 10 minutes left, in a second medium stockpot heat 1 gallon (3.79 liters) water to 170°F (77°C). After the grains have steeped for 60 minutes, turn the heat to high and stir until the temperature reaches 170°F (77°C). Turn off the heat.

SPARGE Place a fine-mesh strainer over a stockpot and pour the grains into the strainer, reserving the liquid. Pour the 1 gallon (3.79 liters) of 170°F (77°C) water over the grains. Recirculate the collected liquid through the grains once.

BOIL Return the pot with the liquid to the stove and bring to a boil over high heat. When the liquid starts to foam, reduce the heat to a slow rolling boil and add the dandelion leaves. Add the black peppercorns after 15 minutes and the lemon peel after 50 minutes. Prepare an ice bath by stopping the sink and filling it halfway with water and ice. At the 60-minute mark, turn off the heat. Place the pot in the ice bath and cool to 70°F (21°C), about 30 minutes.

FERMENT Using a funnel and a strainer, pour the liquid into a sanitized fermenter. Add water as needed to fill the jug to the 1-gallon mark. Add the yeast, sanitize your hands, cover the mouth of the jug with one hand, and shake to distribute evenly. Attach a sanitized stopper and tubing to the fermenter and insert the other end of the tubing into a small bowl of sanitizing solution. The solution will begin to bubble as the yeast activates, pushing gas through the tube. Wait 2 to 3 days, until the bubbling has slowed, then replace the tubing system with an airlock. Wait 11 more days, then bottle, using the honey (see page 13 for bottling instructions).

//

SUGGESTED FOOD PAIRINGS Dandelion greens salad, tomatoes drizzled with olive oil and sea salt, roasted branzino

FOR 5 GALLONS

60-MINUTE MASH AT 152°F (67°C)
2½ gallons (9.46 liters) water, plus 5 gallons (18.93 liters) for sparging; 8 pounds (3628.74 grams) Belgian Pilsner malt; 1.25 pounds (566.99 grams) White Wheat malt

60-MINUTE BOIL 35 dandelion leaves; 5 table-spoons (50 grams) whole black peppercorns; peel from 5 lemons

FERMENT Belgian ale yeast, such as Safbrew T-58; 1 cup (340 grams) honey, for bottling

JENLAIN

JENLAIN, FRANCE

BREWERY

We went to northern France with one question: What makes French beer, well, French? We were first introduced to Jenlain's Ambre over dinner at DBGB's in New York City, and we fell in love with it. It's delicate and malty in a way that tastes like tiny specks of crystallized caramel on the tongue, and it starts and finishes with a gentle spicy aroma that pops off its surface and into your nose. But in the end, it just tastes French, somehow. It is meant to be served with food—good food.

When we saw the style, known as a bière de garde ("beer for keeping"), appearing in American craft breweries, we ordered away, but something was always a bit off. Not that they weren't good beers, because they were—but there was always something too sweet or too bitter, out of balance, or just not French about what we were ordering.

Our only option was traveling to the source to see how it was made.

As the fourth-generation proprietor of a brewery nearing its centennial, Raymond Duyck doesn't talk about the history of his brewery in terms of decades but rather in terms of wars, occupations, industrial and culinary revolutions, and the evolving landscape of northern France.

When the brewery started in 1922 it was one of two thousand breweries in the north of France. These were all farm breweries: Farms first, but in the winter when

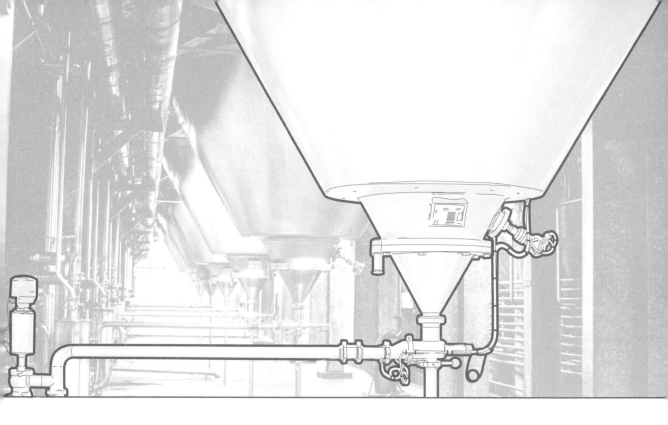

there weren't enough crops to tend, they switched to making beer. They brewed in the colder temperatures of winter and kept the beer in barrels to drink the rest of the year. And what these farms grew, in large part, was barley.

What we found in Jenlain wasn't the quaint, pastoral farmhouse brewery we imagined. It was modernized and dedicated not only to preserving France's beer history but also to expanding it. The brewery purchased and later opened up its canning lines to other breweries that did not have their own. "French beers are unknown all over the world," says Duyck, whose childhood bedroom now serves as his office. Looking out at a landscape of beer drinkers largely unaware that a French beer style even exists, he plays the role of ambassador. "We have to change the idea of the French beer." We think that change starts with a sip.

EXPANDING FRENCH BEER

JENLAIN OPENED UP ITS CANNING LINES TO OTHER BREWERIES THAT DID NOT HAVE THEIR OWN.

BIÈRE DE GARDE

6.15% ABV

60-MINUTE MASH AT 152°F (67°C)

2½ qt (2.37 l) water, plus 1 gal (3.79 l) for sparging

2 lb (907.19 g) French Pale malt

0.3 lb (136.08 g) French Caramel Amber malt

*All grains should be milled (see page 15).

60-MINUTE BOIL

0.5 oz (14.17 g) Strisselspalt hops, divided into fifths

FERMENT

French or Belgian ale yeast, such as Wyeast French Saison or Safale S-33 (see note, page 16)

3 Tbsp (63 g) honey, for bottling

OUR TAKE ON THIS FRENCH CLASSIC RELIES ON FRENCH MALTS AND HOPS AS WELL AS AN EXTENDED BOTTLE AGING TO DEVELOP *UN ÉQUILIBRE PARFAIT,* OR A PERFECT BALANCE. ITS SPICY HOP AROMA REMAINS BRIGHT AS THE MALTS' SWEETNESS MELLOWS OVER TIME. DON'T DRINK ALL YOUR BOTTLES AT ONCE. INSTEAD, ENJOY A FEW HERE AND THERE THROUGHOUT THE YEAR TO HELP YOU APPRECIATE THE TIME WHEN HAVING A BEER CELLAR WASN'T A LUXURY, BUT A NECESSITY. AT LEAST YOU DON'T NEED A GRAIN SILO.

///

MASH In a medium stockpot, heat 2½ quarts (2.37 liters) water over high heat to 160°F (70°C). Add all the malts and stir gently. The temperature should reduce to 150°F (66°C) within 1 minute. Turn off the heat. Steep the grains for 60 minutes between 144°F and 152°F (62°C and 67°C). Every 10 minutes, stir and take the temperature. If the grains get too cold, turn the heat to high and stir until the temperature rises to that range, then turn off the heat. With 10 minutes left, in a second medium stockpot heat 1 gallon (3.79 liters) water to 170°F (77°C). After the grains have steeped for 60 minutes, turn the heat to high and stir until the temperature reaches 170°F (77°C). Turn off the heat.

SPARGE Place a fine-mesh strainer over a stock-pot and pour the grains into the strainer, reserving the liquid. Pour the 1 gallon (3.79 liters) of 170°F (77°C) water over the grains. Recirculate the collected liquid through the grains once.

BOIL Return the pot with the liquid to the stove and bring to a boil over high heat. When the liquid starts to foam, reduce the heat to a slow rolling boil and add two fifths of the Strisselspalt hops. Add another fifth of the hops after 15 and 45 minutes. Prepare an ice bath by stopping the sink and filling it halfway with water and ice. At the 60-minute mark, turn off the heat and add the remaining hops. Place the pot in the ice bath and cool to 70°F (21°C), about 30 minutes.

FERMENT Using a funnel and a strainer, pour the liquid into a sanitized fermenter. Add water as needed to fill the jug to the 1-gallon mark. Add the yeast, sanitize your hands, cover the mouth of the jug with one hand, and shake to distribute evenly. Attach a sanitized stopper and tubing to the fermenter and insert the other end of the tubing into a small bowl of sanitizing solution. The solution will begin to bubble as the yeast activates, pushing gas through the tube. Wait 2 to 3 days, until the bubbling has slowed, then replace the tubing system with an airlock. Wait 11 more days, then bottle, using the honey (see page 13 for bottling instructions).

//

SUGGESTED FOOD PAIRINGS Frisée aux lardons, washed-rind cow's-milk cheese, quiche

FOR 5 GALLONS
60-MINUTE MASH AT 152°F (67°C)
3¼ gallons (12.3 liters) water, plus 5 gallons (15.14 liters) for sparging; 10 pounds (4535.92 grams) French Pale malt; 1.5 pounds (680.38 grams) French Caramel Amber malt

60-MINUTE BOIL 2.5 ounces (70.87 grams) Strisselspalt hops, divided into fifths

FERMENT French or Belgian ale yeast, such as Wyeast French Saison or Safale S-33; 1 cup (340 grams) honey, for bottling

PAUSA CAFE

SALUZZO, ITALY

BREWERY

At Pausa Cafe, in the Piedmont region, the brewers and brewing process are completely cut off from the outside world. Much like the monks who craft the finest Trappist ales, the brewers have no tours, no tasting room, no interaction with the delivery men. Once inside the brewery there is no interaction with anyone except the three brewers who make the beer.

But we were not in a monastery. We were in prison.

Going to prison in a foreign country where the only words you can speak confidently are *grazie* and *birra* is not advisable. But when we became enamored with a beer brewed nearly 4,000 miles away, the metal bars, guards, and metal detectors didn't seem to matter.

All that came to mind was finding Pausa Cafe, the multiprison collective tasked with instilling in inmates skills that are transferable to the outside world. The brewery (manned by two non-prison-bound brewers and one inmate who has been with them since 2006) is located in a penitentiary in orchard-laced Saluzzo, Italy.

Their beers are delicate, fresh, and beautifully balanced—easily fitting the setting beyond the prison walls, where orchards line the nearby roads and stand in stark contrast to what lies inside. But our visit was more than simply a chance to learn about their unique beers produced in a unique environment; it was transformative.

The original bottle of Pausa beer that we picked up in Manhattan's Lower East Side was another man's message in a bottle received on a continent across the world. "When I see these beers going so far away, I can go inside my head and picture the outside world," said Stefano, a prisoner turned brewer.

Gabriel Genduso, the assistant brewer, said it best: "I came here to get an education in brewing, but getting to meet and work with this special person—that was a lesson in humanity."

"WHEN I SEE THESE BEERS GOING SO FAR AWAY, I CAN GO INSIDE MY HEAD AND PICTURE THE OUTSIDE WORLD."

—STEFANO,
BREWER AND INMATE

TAPIOCA ALE

6% ABV

60-MINUTE MASH AT 152°F (67°C)

2¼ qt (2.13 l) water, plus 1 gal (3.79 l) for sparging

1.5 lb (680.39 g) English Pale malt

0.25 lb (113.4 g) Munich malt

0.15 lb (68.04 g) tapioca

0.15 lb (68.04 g) Caramel 40 malt

0.05 lb (22.68 g) Caramel 15 malt

*All grains should be milled (see page 15).

60-MINUTE BOIL

0.4 oz (11.34 g) Styrian Golding hops, divided into thirds

0.2 oz (5.67 g) Glacier hops

FERMENT

English ale yeast, such as Safale S-04 (see note, page 16)

3 Tbsp (63 g) honey, for bottling

TAPIOCA COMES FROM THE ROOT OF THE CASSAVA PLANT, BUT WE TEND TO ASSOCIATE IT MORE WITH BUBBLE TEA AND PUDDING THAN ROOT VEGETABLES. BEER NEVER EVEN ENTERS THE PICTURE, BUT WHY NOT? IT'S A STARCH. STARCHES TURN INTO SUGAR, AND SUGAR BECOMES ALCOHOL. INSPIRED BY PAUSA CAFE'S TAQUAMARI, WHICH FEATURES TAPIOCA IN THE MASH, WE MADE OUR OWN BEER THAT'S EASY-DRINKING WITH A LIGHT, HAZY BODY AND FRESH, PLEASANT FINISH.

MASH In a medium stockpot, heat 2¼ quarts (2.13 liters) water over high heat to 160°F (70°C). Add all the malts and tapioca and stir gently. The temperature should reduce to 150°F (66°C) within 1 minute. Turn off the heat. Steep the grains for 60 minutes between 144°F and 152°F (62°C and 67°C). Every 10 minutes, stir and take the temperature. If the grains get too cold, turn the heat to high and stir until the temperature rises to that range, then turn off the heat. With 10 minutes left, in a second medium stockpot heat 1 gallon (3.79 liters) water to 170°F (77°C). After the grains have steeped for 60 minutes, turn the heat to high and stir until the temperature reaches 170°F (77°C). Turn off the heat.

SPARGE Place a fine-mesh strainer over a stockpot and pour the grains into the strainer, reserving the liquid. Pour the 1 gallon (3.79 liters) of 170°F (77°C) water over the grains. Recirculate the collected liquid through the grains once.

BOIL Return the pot with the liquid to the stove and bring to a boil over high heat. When the liquid starts to foam, reduce the heat to a slow rolling boil and add one third of the Styrian Golding hops. Add the remaining two thirds Styrian Golding hops after 40 minutes and the Glacier hops after 55 minutes. Prepare an ice bath by stopping the sink and filling it halfway with water and ice. At the 60-minute mark, turn off the heat. Place the pot in the ice bath and cool to 70°F (21°C), about 30 minutes.

FERMENT Using a funnel and a strainer, pour the liquid into a sanitized fermenter. Add water as needed to fill the jug to the 1-gallon mark. Add the yeast, sanitize your hands, cover the mouth of the jug with one hand, and shake to distribute evenly. Attach a sanitized stopper and tubing to the fermenter and insert the other end of the tubing into a small bowl of sanitizing solution. The solution will begin to bubble as the yeast activates, push-ing gas through the tube. Wait 2 to 3 days, until the bubbling has slowed, then replace the tubing system with an airlock. Wait 11 more days, then bottle, using the honey (see page 13 for bottling instructions).

//

SUGGESTED FOOD PAIRINGS Tapioca pudding, panna cotta, cured sausage

FOR 5 GALLONS
60-MINUTE MASH AT 152°F (67°C)
2¾ gallons (10.41 liters) water, plus 5 gallons (18.93 liters) for sparging; 7.5 pounds (3401.94 grams) English Pale malt; 1.25 pounds (566.99 grams) Munich malt; 0.75 pound (340.19 grams) tapioca; 0.75 pound (340.19 grams) Caramel 40 malt; 0.25 pound (113.4 grams) Caramel 15 malt

60-MINUTE BOIL
2 ounces (56.7 grams) Styrian Golding hops, divided into thirds; 1 ounce (28.35 grams) Glacier hops

FERMENT English ale yeast, such as Safale S-04; 1 cup (340 grams) honey, for bottling

THE KERNEL

LONDON, ENGLAND

BREWERY

Underneath a series of railway arches in the Bermondsey neighborhood of South London, an artisan food movement has taken hold. Coffee roasters, butchers, and ice cream makers have taken up residence within the narrow rail supports to make their goods. These young producers open their doors on Saturdays in true market fashion and dole out handmade gastronomic delights.

We love markets. We started Brooklyn Brew Shop out of a 10-by-10-foot pop-up tent at the Brooklyn Flea and have a special bond with the picklers, bakers, and candy makers you find there. So when we heard about The Kernel, a brewery that launched out of a railway arch and was brewing up American-style beers, we had to check it out.

The small staff, led by Evin O'Riordain, is built around each person's tasting palate. Their backgrounds are in wine, cheese, and beer, not in engineering or science. What O'Riordain looked for in growing his still-small staff were people who took a taste approach to beer and who were really good at picking apart flavors. For The Kernel, beer is always and most importantly about taste: "It's just about having confidence in your own taste buds and experimenting with different flavors."

It was that interest in flavor profiles, building confidence, and expanding their education as young brew-

ers that led them to make single hop beers over and over again with American, Australian, and New Zealand hops. And also because they just loved fresh, clean, well-hopped beers, which were not easy to find in cask-dominated London.

You won't find them trucking their beers across the Atlantic or even across the UK. Kernel's hop-forward beers should be consumed fresh. If you find yourself just south of the River Thames early on a Saturday morning, however, listen for the sound of the overground rail, and like a hound on the hunt, follow the aromas of cured meats, aged cheeses, and fermenting beer for a local taste of London at its best.

"IT'S JUST ABOUT HAVING CONFIDENCE IN YOUR OWN TASTE BUDS AND EXPERIMENTING WITH DIFFERENT FLAVORS."

—EVIN O'RIORDAIN, *HEAD BREWER*

CHINOOK SINGLE HOP IPA

6.5% ABV

60-MINUTE MASH AT 152°F (67°C)

2½ qt (2.37 l) water, plus 1 gal (3.79 l) for sparging

1.8 lb (816.47 g) English Pale malt

0.4 lb (181.44 g) Caramel 20 malt

0.2 lb (90.72 g) Victory malt

*All grains should be milled (see page 15).

60-MINUTE BOIL

0.42 oz (11.91 g) Chinook hops, divided into sixths

FERMENT

American ale yeast, such as Safale S-05 (see note, page 16)

3 Tbsp (63 g) honey, for bottling

INSPIRED BY THE KERNEL'S AMERICAN-STYLE SINGLE HOP IPAS, WE DECIDED TO BREW UP A SINGLE HOP IPA OF OUR OWN USING FRESH AND CITRUSY AMERICAN HOPS WITH MALTY ENGLISH GRAINS FOR A BALANCED, RICHLY AROMATIC PALE ALE.

///

MASH In a medium stockpot, heat 2½ quarts (2.37 liters) water over high heat to 160°F (70°C). Add all the malts and stir gently. The temperature should reduce to 150°F within 1 minute. Turn off the heat. Steep the grains for 60 minutes between 144°F and 152°F (62°C and 67°C). Every 10 minutes, stir and take the temperature. If the grains get too cold, turn the heat to high and stir until the temperature rises to that range, then turn off the heat. With 10 minutes left, in a second medium stockpot heat 1 gallon (3.79 liters) water to 170°F (77°C). After the grains have steeped for 60 minutes, turn the heat to high and stir until the temperature reaches 170°F (77°C). Turn off the heat.

SPARGE Place a fine-mesh strainer over a stockpot and pour the grains into the strainer, reserving the liquid. Pour the 1 gallon (3.79 liters) of 170°F (77°C) water over the grains. Recirculate the collected liquid through the grains once.

BOIL Return the pot with the liquid to the stove and bring to a boil over high heat. When the liquid starts to foam, reduce the heat to a slow rolling boil and add one sixth of the Chinook hops. Add another sixth of the Chinook hops after 15 minutes, 30 minutes, 45 minutes, and 55 minutes into the boil. Prepare an ice bath by stopping the sink and filling it halfway with water and ice. At the 60-minute mark, turn off the heat and add the remaining sixth Chinook hops. Place the pot in the ice bath and cool to 70°F (21°C), about 30 minutes.

FERMENT Using a funnel and a strainer, pour the liquid into a sanitized fermenter. Add water as needed to fill the jug to the 1-gallon mark. Add the yeast, sanitize your hands, cover the mouth of the jug with one hand, and shake to distribute evenly. Attach a sanitized stopper and tubing to the fermenter and insert the other end of the tubing into a small bowl of sanitizing solution. The solution will begin to bubble as the yeast activates, pushing gas through the tube. Wait 2 to 3 days, until the bubbling has slowed, then replace the tubing system with an airlock. Wait 11 more days, then bottle, using the honey (see page 13 for bottling instructions).

//

SUGGESTED FOOD PAIRINGS Endive salad, raclette (ideally from Borough Market's Kappacasein), seared flank steak

FOR 5 GALLONS
60-MINUTE MASH AT 152°F (67°C)
3¼ gallons (12.3 liters) water, plus 5 gallons (15.14 liters) for sparging; 9 pounds (4082.33 grams) English Pale malt; 2 pounds (907.19 grams) Caramel 20 malt; 1 pound (453.59 grams) Victory malt

60-MINUTE BOIL 2.3 ounces (65.2 grams) Chinook hops, divided into sixths

FERMENT American ale yeast, such as Safale S-05; 1 cup (340 grams) honey, for bottling

VARIATIONS

SINGLE HOP IPA: CITRA
For a blast of tropical fruit on the nose, replace the Chinook hops with 0.5 ounce (14.17 grams) Citra hops; 2.5 ounces (70.87 grams) for the 5-gallon variation.

SINGLE HOP IPA: PACIFICA
To get the full citrusy effect of New Zealand's Pacifica hops, replace the Chinook hops with 0.9 ounce (25.51 grams) Pacifica hops; 4.5 ounces (127.57 grams) for the 5-gallon variation.

CARTON BREWING

ATLANTIC HIGHLANDS, NJ

BREWERY

When Augie Carton and his cousin Chris opened a brewery in a nondescript building that once served as a beer warehouse in their sleepy hometown of Atlantic Highlands on the Jersey Shore, they described what is now their tasting room to be a "soulless box" clad in carpet tiles, white vinyl walls, and drop ceilings. It was the first space they saw, but they took it.

Heavy rain and an old, leaky roof led them to realize something about their box. Above the drop ceiling dripping with water were exposed wooden beams and a skylight. Behind the white vinyl walls was beautiful old brick. Beneath the carpet tile was a wooden floor. Jeremy, a brewer, asked his father to build a bar, and a tasting room was born.

And that tasting room is the best place to sample their low-alcohol, highly sessionable beers. These beers, as Augie describes them, aren't so much "seasonal," because they are not likely to return the following season, but rather "specials" based on a collective whim.

Augie, Chris, and the brewers gather on Sundays, kick ideas around, and brew up the most interesting idea they come up with on the pilot system before committing to a fairly small 15-barrel batch. The rules are simple: They want to make beers they have not had, beers that have not been made, beers that evolve with every sip, and beers that ultimately stick to an ABV low enough to permit you to have more than one.

MULBERRY WHEAT

5.5% ABV

60-MINUTE MASH AT 152°F (67°C)

2 qt (1.89 l) water, plus 1.2 gal (4.54 l) for sparging

1.2 lb (544.31 g) American 2-row malt

0.6 lb (272.16 g) Pale Wheat malt

0.3 lb (136.08 g) Munich malt

*All grains should be milled (see page 15).

60-MINUTE BOIL

0.4 oz (11.34 g) Styrian Golding hops, divided into quarters

1 pt (200 g) mulberries

FERMENT

Wheat ale yeast, such as Safbrew WB-06 (see note, page 16)

3 Tbsp (63 g) honey, for bottling

BACK IN BROOKLYN AND ENAMORED WITH THE IDEA OF FORAGED INGREDIENTS (SEE FULLSTEAM, PAGE 118), WE SET OUT TO FIND SOMETHING GROWING WILD IN THE CITY TO PUT INTO OUR NEXT BATCH. WE RESEARCHED CITY FORAGING AND SIGNED UP FOR A PROSPECT PARK FORAGING TOUR THAT ENDED UP GETTING CANCELED FOR LACK OF INTEREST AND LACK OF FORAGEABLES IN THE STILL TOO-EARLY SPRING.

SO WE DISMISSED THE IDEA OF RAMPS OR FIDDLEHEADS AND FOCUSED ON OTHER ATTAINABLE BREWS INSTEAD. COME JUNE, WHEN WE SET UP A TABLE IN THE BACKYARD, MULBERRIES STARTED HITTING US ON THE HEAD AND WE REALIZED EXACTLY WHAT OUR FORAGER BEER SHOULD BE.

CARTON BREWING'S MONKEY CHASED THE WEASEL, A SUPER-TART, MULBERRY-LACED BERLINER WEISSE, WAS ALSO BORN OF AN OVERACTIVE MULBERRY TREE IN CLOSE PROXIMITY TO A BREW KETTLE. OUR VERSION IS SOFTER (MULBERRIES AREN'T PARTICULARLY TART), BUT YOU COULD CERTAINLY ADD THEM TO THE BERLINER WEISSE (PAGE 22) FOR A MORE SOUR TAKE.

(continued on next page)

MASH In a medium stockpot, heat 2 quarts (1.89 liters) water over high heat to 160°F (70°C). Add all the malts and stir gently. The temperature should reduce to 150°F (66°C) within 1 minute. Turn off the heat. Steep the grains for 60 minutes between 144°F and 152°F (62°C and 67°C). Every 10 minutes, stir and take the temperature. If the grains get too cold, turn the heat to high and stir until the temperature rises to that range, then turn off the heat. With 10 minutes left, in a second medium stockpot heat 1.2 gallons (4.54 liters) water to 170°F (77°C). After the grains have steeped for 60 minutes, turn the heat to high and stir until the temperature reaches 170°F (77°C). Turn off the heat.

SPARGE Place a fine-mesh strainer over a stockpot and pour the grains into the strainer, reserving the liquid. Pour the 1.2 gallons (4.54 liters) of 170°F (77°C) water over the grains. Recirculate the collected liquid through the grains once.

BOIL Return the pot with the liquid to the stove and bring to a boil over high heat. When the liquid starts to foam, reduce the heat to a slow rolling boil and add half the Styrian Golding hops. Add one fourth of the hops after 30 minutes. Add the remaining hops after 55 minutes. Prepare an ice bath by stopping the sink and filling it halfway with water and ice. At the 60-minute mark, turn off the heat and add the mulberries. Place the pot in the ice bath and cool to 70°F (21°C), about 30 minutes.

FERMENT Using a funnel and a strainer, pour the liquid into a sanitized fermenter. Add water as needed to fill the jug to the 1-gallon mark. Add the yeast, sanitize your hands, cover the mouth of the jug with one hand, and shake to distribute evenly. Attach a sanitized stopper and tubing to the fermenter and insert the other end of the tubing into a small bowl of sanitizing solution. The solution will begin to bubble as the yeast activates, pushing gas through the tube. Wait 2 to 3 days, until the bubbling has slowed, then replace the tubing system with an airlock. Wait 11 more days, then bottle, using the honey (see page 13 for bottling instructions).

//

SUGGESTED FOOD PAIRINGS Soft-shell crabs, corn chowder, Shandy Ice Pops (page 97)

BACKYARD VARIATIONS

WILD BLUEBERRY WHEAT

For those lucky enough to forage in Maine, wild blueberries are your reward. Replace mulberries with 1 pint (400 grams) blueberries; 2.5 quarts (2000 grams) for the 5-gallon variation.

HUCKLEBERRY WHEAT

Tart, sweet, and a favorite of bears, huckleberries grow abundantly west of the Rocky Mountains. Replace mulberries with 1 pint (400 grams) huckleberries; 2.5 quarts (2000 grams) for the 5-gallon variation.

PRICKLY PEAR WHEAT

Deserts aren't known for their sweet and juicy produce, but there are a few rare exceptions. Prickly pear, also known as cactus fruit, is one of those exceptions. Its mild, berrylike sweetness makes it a subtle companion to an otherwise pleasant blonde ale. Replace mulberries with 1 pint (320 grams) prickly pear chopped into ½ inch cubes; 2.5 quarts (1600 grams) for the 5-gallon variation. Replace the honey with equal amounts agave when bottling.

LINGONBERRY WHEAT

Not the tastiest berry picked fresh off the bush, lingonberries are normally relegated to the realm of Scandinavian jams, but can add a subtle tartness and slightly pink hue to a light Belgian-style beer. Replace mulberries with 1 pint (400 grams) lingonberries; 2.5 quarts (2000 grams) for the 5-gallon variation.

FOR 5 GALLONS

60-MINUTE MASH AT 152°F (67°C)

2½ gallons (9.46 liters) water, plus 6 gallons (22.71 liters) for sparging; 6 pounds (2721.55 grams) American 2-row malt; 3 pounds (1360.78 grams) Pale Wheat malt; 1.5 pounds (680.39 grams) Munich malt

60-MINUTE BOIL 2 ounces (56.7 grams)

Styrian Golding hops, divided into quarters; 2.5 quarts (1000 grams) mulberries

FERMENT Wheat ale yeast, such as Safbrew WB-06; 1 cup (340 grams) honey, for bottling

It's not every day that you discover a lost beer style. Anthropologists and historians spend their lives uncovering history's mysteries under centuries of decay or buried within forgotten jungles. Gose could have been one of those secrets waiting for its whip-wielding college-professor-turned-adventurer to save it from the depths of antiquity, but it's not lost today in large part because of some people working in a converted train station in Leipzig.

Gose is an old German beer style that traditionally was brewed with coriander and salt with a spontaneous lactic fermentation. Imagine some of the same microscopic critters behind yogurt and a variety of cheeses focusing their attention on beer. The result is a tart, mildly funky, subtly spicy, light-bodied German ale with a hint of saltiness.

Although the style disappeared a few times from active production in the twentieth century, it began flowing again in 2000 with the renovation and opening of Gasthaus & Gosebrauerei Bayerischer Bahnhof, a brewery housed in what was once a train station. A few things have changed since the eighteenth century. As gose slowly gains in popularity among craft brewers worldwide, you'll find a range of sources and salt levels from nonexistent to Dead Sea heights. Leipzig errs on the lighter side of salinity. The method for adding tartness has also changed over time, ranging from the simple addition of lactic acid (as in Leipzig) to a full-on sour mash.

When the history of beer can be tasted, it won't die away. Even the most obscure recipe can stay alive. It can be brewed again, and what was once known by only one town in one country at a specific point in time can join the greater brewing culture worldwide.

Whether in a converted train station or a garage in Golden, Colorado (where we had our first gose), brewers have decided that gose isn't going away. The flavors may be all over the map, but so are the breweries that have decided to take what was the local beer of choice in one German city more than a century ago and make it their own.

AS GOSE SLOWLY GAINS IN POPULARITY AMONG CRAFT BREWERS WORLDWIDE, YOU'LL FIND A RANGE OF SOURCES, AND SALT LEVELS FROM NONEXISTENT TO DEAD SEA HEIGHTS.

CELERY SALT GOSE

5.6% ABV

PREP

1 cup (0.24 l) water

0.2 lb (90.72 g) German Pilsner malt

45-MINUTE MASH AT 152°F (67°C)

2 qt (1.89 l) water, plus 1 gal (3.79 l) for sparging

1 lb (453.59 g) German Pilsner malt

0.6 lb (272.16 g) Pale Wheat malt

0.3 lb (136.08 g) Vienna malt

0.3 lb (136.08 g) acidulated malt

*All grains should be milled (see page 15).

60-MINUTE BOIL

0.1 oz (2.83 g) Challenger hops, divided in half

0.3 oz (8.5 g) Spaltz hops, divided into thirds

1 tsp (3 g) celery salt

FERMENT

Wheat ale yeast, such as Safbrew WB-06 (see note, page 16)

3 Tbsp (63 g) honey, for bottling

A GOSE PAIRS WELL WITH FOOD. LOTS OF BEERS DO (SEE ANY OF OUR FOOD PAIRINGS THROUGHOUT THIS BOOK), BUT THERE'S SOMETHING ABOUT THE LEIPZIG CLASSIC THAT BRINGS IT A LITTLE CLOSER TO THE TABLE. IT'S GOT SO MUCH THAT MOST BEERS DON'T BY DEFAULT. IT'S A LITTLE BRINY. IT'S ALSO A LITTLE TART. WE GET THAT FROM A PARTIAL SOUR MASH, WHICH KEEPS IT WELL SHY OF A BLUE CHEESE STINK BUT FIRMLY WITHIN THE BOUNDS OF FUNKY TOWN. THE ADDITION OF SALT HELPS IT APPROACH UMAMI, THE SAVORY TASTE IN ALL THINGS DELICIOUS. FOR OUR VERSION WE WENT WITH CELERY SALT, GIVING IT A FRESH, MILDLY VEGETAL QUALITY THAT PLAYS NICELY WITH THE BEER'S HERBAL, SPICY HOPS.

PREP Three days before brewing, heat 1 cup (0.24 liter) water in a small pot over high heat to 130°F (54°C). Turn off the heat, add the 0.2 pound (90.72 grams) of German Pilsner malt, and stir gently. The temperature should reduce to 120°F (49°C) within 1 minute. Cover the pot and steep the grains for 45 minutes at 120°F (49°C). Every 10 minutes, stir and take the temperature. If the grains get too cold, turn the heat to high and stir until the temperature rises to 120°F (49°C). After 45 minutes, cover the surface of the grains with plastic wrap so no air touches the grains and leave for 3 days in a spot that reaches 115°F (46°C), such as over a radiator or space heater or in a gas oven with only the pilot light on. This is how to make a "sour mash."

MASH In a medium stockpot, heat 2 quarts (1.89 liters) water over high heat to 160°F (70°C). Add all the malts and stir gently. The temperature should reduce to 150°F (66°C) within 1 minute. Turn off the heat. Steep the grains for 45 minutes between 144°F and 152°F (62°C and 67°C). Every 10 minutes, stir and take the temperature. If the grains get too cold, turn the heat to high and stir until the temperature rises to that range, then turn off the heat. With 10 minutes left, in a second medium stockpot heat 1 gallon (3.79 liters) water to 170°F (77°C). After the grains have steeped for 60 minutes, turn the heat to high and stir until the temperature reaches 170°F (77°C). Turn off the heat.

SPARGE Place a fine-mesh strainer over a stockpot and pour the grains (including those from the sour mash) into the strainer, reserving the liquid. Pour the 1 gallon (3.79 liters) of 170°F (77°C) water over the grains. Recirculate the collected liquid through the grains once.

BOIL Return the pot with the liquid to the stove and bring to a boil over high heat. When the liquid starts to foam, reduce the heat to a slow rolling boil and add half of the Challenger hops. Add the remaining Challenger hops after 30 minutes. Add one third of the Spaltz hops after 45 minutes and another third after 55 minutes. Prepare an ice bath by stopping the sink and filling it halfway with water and ice. At the 60-minute mark, turn off the heat and add the remaining third of Spaltz hops and the celery salt, stirring to dissolve the salt. Place the pot in the ice bath and cool to 70°F (21°C), about 30 minutes.

FERMENT Using a funnel and a strainer, pour the liquid into a sanitized fermenter. Add water as needed to fill the jug to the 1-gallon mark. Add the yeast, sanitize your hands, cover the mouth of the jug with one hand, and shake to distribute evenly. Attach a sanitized stopper and tubing to the fermenter and insert the other end of the tubing into a small bowl of sanitizing solution. The solution will begin to bubble as the yeast activates, pushing gas through the tube. Wait 2 to 3 days, until the bubbling has slowed, then replace the tubing system with an airlock. Wait 11 more days, then bottle, using the honey (see page 13 for bottling instructions).

//

SUGGESTED FOOD PAIRINGS Baked eggs, bacon-wrapped trout, quiche

FOR 5 GALLONS
PREP 5 cups (1.18 liters) water; 1 pound (453.59 grams) German Pilsner malt

45-MINUTE MASH AT 152°F (67°C)
2½ gallons (9.46 liters) water, plus 5 gallons (18.93 liters) for sparging; 5 pounds (2267.96 grams) German Pilsner malt; 3 pounds (1360.78 grams) Pale Wheat malt; 1.5 pounds (680.39 grams) Vienna malt; 1.5 pounds (680.39 grams) acidulated malt

60-MINUTE BOIL 0.5 ounce (14.17 grams) Challenger hops, divided in half; 1.5 ounces (42.52 grams) Spaltz hops, divided into thirds; 5 teaspoons (15 grams) celery salt

FERMENT Wheat ale yeast, such as Safbrew WB-06; 1 cup (340 grams) honey, for bottling

HILL FARMSTEAD

GREENSBORO BEND, VT

BREWERY

Shaun Hill brews beer in a field in Vermont's Northeast Kingdom. Parking is one of the banes of his existence. Daily troves of local drinkers, curious tourists, and globe-trekking beer hunters park haphazardly on the edges of his family's eighth-generation Greensboro farm to form lines, growlers in hand, for his beer. But this demand wasn't initially anticipated.

Starting a brewery with little more than a modest loan taken out against the property where the family farm has sat for generations is a daunting proposition for anyone starting up a new brewery. This is especially true in a place where nearby farms increasingly add equipment bearing the same sheen as a new car fresh off the lot while others feature rusty pickups and tractors older than we are.

Similar to Hill's start in brewing are the prospects of today's upstart brewers who after years of making beer may one day say "I'm going to go all in and use the $20,000 I've saved up from painting houses for ten years to try to buy some equipment, cobble it together, and try to make two hundred gallons of beer a week and hope someone buys it."

"If they don't I'm going to lose this farm," says Hill, adding, "It's a glorious occupation, right?"

Authenticity is not something that can be learned, and being born on the land where you brew and choose to spend the rest of your life cannot be bought. Still, Hill worries that the world will see the small and slow supply of beer, the missing shingles adorning the brewery's walls, the winding, minimally paved road leading to the brewhouse, and the field that's been in his family for years as the front for a much larger, more commercial, less authentic endeavor.

As we speak, he in turn quotes Dostoevsky, discusses consumerism as a replacement for God, and advises on avoiding the cult of personality. He would prefer that people focus on the beer and not on him. Or at least understand that his focus is on the beers, and not necessarily crowd management (which is why the parking situation gets to him).

And the beers he crafts carry their own authenticity. The majority of them are simple beers, named after his ancestors who farmed this land before him. But it is the expression of these beers, balanced and fragrant, well-hopped but not astringent, that is entirely worth lining up for.

AUTHENTICITY IS NOT SOMETHING THAT CAN BE LEARNED, AND BEING BORN ON THE LAND WHERE YOU BREW AND CHOOSE TO SPEND THE REST OF YOUR LIFE CANNOT BE BOUGHT.

CHAMOMILE BLONDE

5.8% ABV

60-MINUTE MASH AT 152°F (67°C)

2¼ qt (2.27 l) water, plus 1 gal (3.79 l) for sparging

1.5 lb (680.39 g) Belgian Pilsner malt

0.3 lb (136.08 g) Victory malt

0.2 lb (90.72 g) Caramel 10 malt

*All grains should be milled (see page 15).

60-MINUTE BOIL

0.3 oz (8.5 g) Saaz hops, divided into thirds

FERMENT

Belgian ale yeast, such as Safale S-33 (see note, page 16)

3 Tbsp (63 g) honey, for bottling

1 cup (25 g) dried chamomile flowers

AT WTF COFFEE LAB IN FORT GREENE, BROOKLYN, DURING AN EARLY SPRING ESPRESSO WARM-UP WHILE SHOPPING AT THE SATURDAY MORNING FARMER'S MARKET, WE NOTICED SOMETHING INTERESTING. THE BARISTA WAS BUSY POURING WATER SLOWLY AND EVENLY (MUCH LIKE THE SPARGE) THROUGH METAL CONES FOR WHAT WE ASSUMED WAS POUR-OVER COFFEE, UNTIL WE GOT A BETTER LOOK. INSIDE, INSTEAD OF FRESHLY GROUND BEANS, WERE DRIED CHAMOMILE FLOWERS. INTRIGUED, WE REPEATED THE PROCESS AT HOME TO MAKE CHAMOMILE TEA, AND THEN AGAIN TO MAKE THIS BEER THAT HAS ALL THE LOVELY CHAMOMILE AROMATICS WITHOUT ANY OF THE ASTRINGENCY THAT CAN COME WITH OVER-STEEPING.

MASH In a medium stockpot, heat 2¼ quarts (2.27 liters) water over high heat to 160°F (70°C). Add all the malts and stir gently. The temperature should reduce to 150°F (66°C) within 1 minute. Turn off the heat. Steep the grains for 60 minutes between 144°F and 152°F (62°C and 67°C). Every 10 minutes, stir and take the temperature. If the grains get too cold, turn the heat to high and stir until the temperature rises to that range, then turn off the heat. With 10 minutes left, in a second medium stockpot heat 1 gallon water to 170°F (77°C). After the grains have steeped for 60 minutes, turn the heat to high and stir until the temperature reaches 170°F (77°C). Turn off the heat.

SPARGE Place a fine-mesh strainer over a stock-pot and pour the grains into the strainer, reserving the liquid. Pour the 1 gallon (3.79 liters) of 170°F (77°C) water over the grains. Recirculate the collected liquid through the grains once.

BOIL Return the pot with the liquid to the stove and bring to a boil over high heat. When the liquid starts to foam, reduce the heat to a slow rolling boil and add one third of the Saaz hops. Add another third of the hops after 45 minutes and the final third after 55 minutes. Prepare an ice bath by stopping the sink and filling it halfway with water and ice. At the 60-minute mark, turn off the heat. Place the pot in the ice bath and cool to 70°F (21°C), about 30 minutes.

FERMENT Place a strainer over a funnel. Add the chamomile flowers to the strainer, and pour the liquid through the flowers into a sanitized fermenter. Add water as needed to fill the jug to the 1-gallon mark. Add the yeast, sanitize your hands, cover the mouth of the jug with one hand, and shake to distribute evenly. Attach a sanitized stopper and tubing to the fermenter and insert the other end of the tubing into a small bowl of sanitizing solution. The solution will begin to bubble as the yeast activates, pushing gas through the tube.

Wait 2 to 3 days, until the bubbling has slowed, then replace the tubing system with an airlock. Wait 11 more days, then bottle, using the honey (see page 13 for bottling instructions).

//

SUGGESTED FOOD PAIRINGS Spent Grain Popovers (page 58), scones with clotted cream, frittata

FOR 5 GALLONS

60-MINUTE MASH AT 152°F (67°C)
2.8 gallons (10.65 liters) water, plus 5 gallons (18.93 liters) for sparging; 7.5 pounds (3401.94 grams) Belgian Pilsner malt; 1.5 pounds (680.38 grams) Victory malt; 1 pound (453.59 grams) Caramel 10 malt

60-MINUTE BOIL
1.5 ounces (42.52 grams) Saaz hops, divided into thirds

FERMENT Belgian ale yeast, such as Safale S-33; 1 cup (340 grams) honey, for bottling; 5 cups (125 grams) dried chamomile flowers

IPA HUMMUS

MAKES 4 CUPS

2 15.5-oz (430-g) cans chickpeas, drained and well rinsed

3 garlic cloves, minced

½ cup (0.12 l) tahini

Juice of 1 lemon

1 tsp (6 g) kosher salt, plus more to taste

½ tsp (3 g) cayenne

Crushed black pepper to taste

½ cup (0.12 l) IPA

ALTHOUGH WE BREW A LOT OF IPAS (SEE CHINOOK SINGLE HOP IPA, PAGE 38; IPA, BELGIAN STYLE, PAGE 76; SIX HOP IPA, PAGE 116; AND WARRIOR DOUBLE IPA, PAGE 162), WE DON'T OFTEN COOK WITH THEM. THE BRIGHT ZINGY CITRUS AND PINE NOTES THAT DOMINATE OUR FAVORITE IPAS ARE BROKEN DOWN QUICKLY BY HEAT DURING COOKING, LEAVING ONLY THE BITTERNESS BEHIND.

THAT'S WHY THE IDEA OF AN IPA HUMMUS WAS SO REFRESHING—WITH ONLY A MINIMAL AMOUNT OF HEAT NEEDED FOR PUREEING, THOSE REFRESHING CITRUS NOTES WOULD REMAIN. THE RESULT IS A FANTASTIC SMOOTH AND CREAMY HUMMUS WITH A TOUCH OF CITRUS HOP BITTERNESS AND ZING.

1 Combine all the ingredients except for the beer in a food processor or super-strength blender. Blend. Stream the beer in slowly and blend to a rough puree, occasionally scraping down the sides, until the desired consistency is reached.

2 Chill for 2 hours to let the flavors meld. Season with additional salt and pepper to taste.

PIMENTO BEER CHEESE

MAKES 2 CUPS

1 lb (425.25 g) cheddar cheese, shredded

8-oz (142-g) jar pimento peppers, drained and chopped

1 cup (0.24 l) mayonnaise

½ cup (0.12 l) light flavorful beer, such as Bruxelles Blonde (page 102)

1 Tbsp (7.81 g) all-purpose flour

Salt and pepper

THE STRUCTURE OF PIMENTO CHEESE IS PRETTY SIMPLE— SHREDDED CHEDDAR, MAYO, AND A JAR OF CHOPPED SWEET PIMENTO PEPPERS—BUT FROM THERE IT SEEMS EVERYONE HAS A TWIST ON SPICES AND ADDITIONS TO MAKE IT THEIR OWN. OUR VERSION USES A LIGHT, FLAVORFUL BEER MELTED INTO A CHEESE SAUCE THAT IS THEN MIXED INTO THE TRADITIONAL BASE FOR A PLEASANT BEERY KICK. AND IF YOU CAN MANAGE TO RESIST EATING THE ENTIRE BOWL IN PURE DIP FORM, IT ALSO MAKES FOR AN AMAZING GRILLED CHEESE SANDWICH.

//

1 Combine two thirds of the shredded cheddar, the pimentos, and mayonnaise in a large bowl. Set aside.

2 In a saucepan over medium-low heat, simmer the beer until it has reduced by half.

3 Toss the remaining third of the cheddar with the flour to coat. In a double boiler, combine the cheddar-flour mixture with the reduced beer and melt the cheese, stirring until smooth. Let cool slightly.

4 Add the cheese sauce to the cheddar, pimento, and mayo mixture. Stir to incorporate. Season with salt and pepper to taste.

5 Refrigerate for 20 minutes to allow the flavors to meld. Enjoy.

BEER FRUIT LEATHER

MAKES 10 FRUIT LEATHER ROLLS

1 apple, peeled, cored, and quartered

½ pt (156 g) raspberries

1 pt (288 g) strawberries

¼ cup (0.06 l) light, flavorful beer (such as Bruxelles Blonde, page 102, or Mulberry Wheat, page 41)

THIS RECIPE WORKS BEST IF YOU HAVE ACCESS TO SOME EQUIPMENT: YOU NEED A REALLY GOOD BLENDER—ONE THAT CAN HANDLE WHOLE FRUITS—AND A DEHYDRATOR WITH FRUIT LEATHER TRAYS. IF YOU DON'T HAVE A FANTASTIC BLENDER OR A FOOD PROCESSOR, YOU CAN SUBSTITUTE APPLESAUCE FOR THE WHOLE APPLE. AND IF YOU DON'T HAVE A DEHYDRATOR, YOU CAN USE YOUR OVEN ON A LOW TEMPERATURE. WE SWAP THE FRUIT FOR WHATEVER THE FARM STAND HAS IN SEASON, AND POUR IN THE LIGHTEST, MOST AROMATIC BEER FROM OUR REFRIGERATOR.

1 Blend all the ingredients in a high-powered blender until pureed. If your blender is not very powerful you can sub in ¼ cup (0.06 liter) applesauce for the apple.

2 If using a dehydrator with fruit leather trays (the smooth plastic inserts), spray the trays with nonstick cooking spray, pour in the pureed fruit, and dehydrate at 135°F (57°C) for 6 to 8 hours until it's dry throughout but not brittle. If using an oven, line a rimmed baking tray with a silicone mat or parchment paper, pour in the pureed fruit, and bake on the lowest oven setting, usually between 170°F and 200°F (77°C and 93°C), for about 6 hours.

3 Cut the fruit leather into strips with a pizza cutter or kitchen shears.

BLACK PEPPER, PARMESAN, AND BEER GRITS

SERVES 8

1½ cups (0.35 l) medium-
  bodied, flavorful beer

1½ cups (0.35 l) water

2 cups (358 g) grits or
  coarse-ground cornmeal
  (not instant grits)

2 Tbsp (28 g) unsalted butter

¾ cup (85 g) shredded Parmesan

1 tsp (6 g) coarsely ground
  black pepper

½ cup (0.12 l) heavy cream

Salt

STIRRING A BIG POT OF GRITS FEELS EXACTLY LIKE STIRRING THE MASH IN BREWING. SO IT ONLY MADE SENSE TO COMBINE THE TWO WITH BEER-SPIKED GRITS. THE KEY TO SUPER-CREAMY GRITS IS COOKING THEM LOW AND SLOW AND ADDING LIQUID THROUGHOUT, ALMOST LIKE A RISOTTO. THEN STIR IN THE PARMESAN AND HEAVY CREAM TO FINISH THEM OFF.

1   In a heavy-bottomed stockpot, bring the beer and water to a boil. Gradually pour in the grits, stirring, and reduce the heat to maintain a low simmer.

2   Simmer the grits over low heat for 1 hour, stirring often and adding more water, ¼ cup (0.06 liter) at a time, as the liquid is fully absorbed.

3   After an hour, or when the grits are tender, remove from the heat and add in the butter, Parmesan, and black pepper, stirring until the butter has melted, then add the heavy cream and stir once more. Season with salt to taste.

SPENT GRAIN PRIMER

Grain is a natural by-product of brewing. After being used, it's called "spent grain." Breweries tend to cart it to local farms for feed, but unless you raise chickens or share a yard with Old MacDonald, you'll have some left over the next time you brew.

FIVE WAYS TO USE SPENT GRAIN

WET Use in hearty loaves of bread or as a substitute for bread crumbs in things like meatballs, veggie burgers, and homemade sausage.

....

DRY Use as a substitute for panko or to top Beer & Bacon Mac & Cheese (page 135). To dry out spent grain:

1 Use a food dehydrator set between 120°F and 130°F (49°C and 54°C) for 8 to 12 hours. Alternatively, dry in your oven at the lowest temperature. For most ovens this is between 170°F and 200°F (77°C and 93°C).

2 Spread out your spent grain on a clean, ungreased sheet pan in a ¼-inch (0.64-centimeter) layer.

3 Place in the oven and let dry for approximately 7 hours, tossing the grain halfway through. Your grain is dry when you feel absolutely no remaining moisture.

4 Store your grain in an airtight jar or plastic container in your pantry.

MILL Use as you would a whole-grain flour to add nuttiness to baked goods. To mill spent grain:

1 Follow the steps for drying spent grain.

2 Using a coffee or spice grinder, process the dried grain until it becomes a fine flour.

3 Store your spent grain flour in an airtight jar or plastic container in your pantry for up to 4 months.

FREEZE Spent grain spoils quickly. So if you don't have the time (or the energy) to use or dry it, your best option is to freeze it in ½-cup servings to use in recipes as needed.

....

COMPOST For those of you who compost, spent grain is pretty much your best friend. The wet grain is considered a "brown" (which normally can only be obtained from decaying leaves in the fall), so using spent grain means you can properly layer and speed up composting year round.

....

SPENT GRAIN NO-RISE PIZZA DOUGH

MAKES 1 LARGE PIZZA

1½ cups (187.5 g) all-purpose flour

¾ cup (0.18 l) dried spent grain (see note)

1 0.25-oz (7-g) package active dry yeast (not ale yeast)

1½ tsp (9.13 g) salt

1 tsp (5 g) sugar

½ cup (0.12 l) warm water, approximately 110°F (43°C), plus more as needed

1 tsp (13.46 g) olive oil

Pizza toppings of your choice

WHEREVER YOU MAY LIVE, THERE IS AN UNDENIABLE AND INEXTRICABLE LINK BETWEEN PIZZA AND BEER. WHERE YOU FIND ONE, YOU ALMOST INVARIABLY FIND THE OTHER, AND THERE'S GOOD REASON FOR IT. JUST AS THE POSSIBILITIES WITH BEER ARE ENDLESS, SO IS PIZZA DOUGH A BLANK SLATE, ABLE TO TAKE ON TOPPINGS THAT AREN'T LIMITED TO ANY ONE SEASON OR NATIONAL CUISINE. WE DECIDED THE ONLY WAY TO DEEPEN THE BOND BETWEEN THESE TWO STAPLES WAS TO MAKE ONE WITH THE OTHER.

//

1 Pulse the flour, spent grain, yeast, salt, and sugar in a food processor until mixed.

2 With the processor running, gradually pour the warm water and olive oil through the feed tube. (If the mixture is too dry, add 1 or 2 more tablespoons warm water.) Process until the dough forms a ball, then process for 1 minute to knead the dough.

3 Transfer the dough to a lightly floured surface. Cover with plastic wrap and let rest for 10 to 15 minutes.

4 While the dough rests, preheat the oven to 450°F (230°C).

5 Place the dough on a half-size sheet pan. Using your hands, stretch the dough evenly over the sheet pan surface. Top with your favorite pizza toppings.

6 Bake for 20 minutes or until the crust is browned and the topping is bubbly.

NOTE If using wet spent grain, reduce the water to ¼ cup (0.06 liter).

SPENT GRAIN POPOVERS

MAKES 8 POPOVERS

¾ cup (96 g) all-purpose flour

¼ cup (32 g) spent grain flour

½ tsp (3 g) salt

2 large eggs

1 cup (0.24 l) milk

2 Tbsp (28 g) unsalted butter, melted

POPOVERS ARE A LITTLE BIT LIKE MAGIC. THE INGREDIENTS FOR THE BATTER ARE AS SIMPLE AS CAN BE (FLOUR, EGG, MILK). YOU CAN SCRAPE EVERYTHING TOGETHER AND INTO THE OVEN IN LESS THAN FIVE MINUTES. BUT THE DELIGHTFULLY CRISP SHELL AND IMPOSSIBLY AIRY, STILL-STEAMING INSIDES MAKE YOU WONDER—IF IT'S REALLY THIS EASY (AND IT IS), WHY AREN'T THESE COMING OUT OF YOUR OVEN EVERY DAY?

THE KEY TO REALLY TALL POPOVERS IS DEFINITELY A PROPER POPOVER PAN. A MUFFIN PAN WILL DELIVER SHORTER (BUT TOTALLY TASTY) VERSIONS. WE ADD JUST A TOUCH OF SPENT GRAIN TO OURS FOR A LIGHT NUTTINESS. AND WHILE WE NORMALLY THINK OF THEM FOR BRUNCH, THIS RECIPE HAS POPOVERS VYING TO BE OUR GO-TO DINNER ROLL.

1   Preheat the oven to 450°F (232°C). When the oven is hot, preheat a popover (or muffin) pan while combining the other ingredients.

2   In a mixing bowl, sift together the flours and salt. Set aside.

3   In a second mixing bowl, whisk together the eggs and milk until combined. Add the wet ingredients to the dry and stir until well blended.

4   Remove the pan from oven and brush with the melted butter. Pour batter halfway up each cup. Bake for 20 minutes. Reduce the heat to 375°F (190°C) and bake for an additional 20 minutes.

SPENT GRAIN PEANUT BUTTER COOKIES

MAKES 24 COOKIES

4 Tbsp (56 g) unsalted butter, softened

½ cup (110 g) packed light brown sugar

1 large egg

⅔ cup (195 g) chunky peanut butter

¼ tsp (1 g) salt

¼ tsp (1 g) baking soda

¼ tsp (1 g) vanilla extract

½ cup (64 g) all-purpose flour

½ cup (64 g) spent grain flour

½ cup (45 g) dried spent grain

THESE PEANUT BUTTER COOKIES PACK A SERIOUS SPENT GRAIN PUNCH. WITH EQUAL PARTS DRIED SPENT GRAIN, SPENT GRAIN FLOUR, AND REGULAR FLOUR, THEY ARE EXTRA NUTTY. WE ALSO USE CHUNKY PEANUT BUTTER RATHER THAN SMOOTH, SO THE DRIED SPENT GRAIN PAIRED WITH THE CHUNKS OF PEANUT CREATES A PLEASANT CRUNCH THROUGHOUT AN OTHERWISE MELT-IN-YOUR-MOUTH COOKIE.

1 Preheat the oven to 375°F (190°C).

2 In a mixing bowl, cream the butter and sugar. Add the egg and beat until combined. Add the remaining ingredients and beat until well blended.

3 Roll spoonfuls of dough into golf-ball-size balls. Place on a baking sheet lined with a silicone baking mat or well-greased cookie sheet. Using a fork, press down each cookie, then rotate the fork 90 degrees and press down again, creating a cross-hatch pattern. Repeat for the rest of the dough.

4 Bake for 12 minutes. Transfer to a cooling rack and let cool for 3 to 5 minutes.

SUMMER
IS FOR
kicking back
WITH BEERS

• ★ • ///////////// • ★ •

Barbecues. Beach days. Vacations. Summertime is for kicking back with refreshing beers that both help beat the heat and complement whatever you're pulling off the grill. These playful recipes pair classic summer saison and farmhouse ale styles with refreshing ingredients.

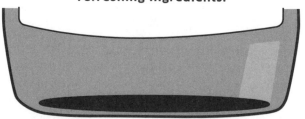

THE BREWERIES
THAT INSPIRED OUR BREWS

RANGER CREEK
BREWING & DISTILLING
(SAN ANTONIO, TX)

**RANGER CREEK'S
MESQUITE SMOKED
PORTER**

CIGAR CITY BREWING
(TAMPA, FL)

CUCUMBER SAISON

LOGSDON ORGANIC
FARMHOUSE ALES
(HOOD RIVER, OR)

FARMHOUSE ALE

JESTER KING
(AUSTIN, TX)

TABLE BEER

BIRRIFICIO MONTEGIOCO
(PIEDMONT, ITALY)

BLENDED FRUIT BEER

WICKED WEED
(ASHEVILLE, NC)

**STRAWBERRY RHUBARB
STRONG ALE**

BREWERY OMMEGANG
(COOPERSTOWN, NY)

IPA, BELGIAN STYLE

BUNKER BREWING
(PORTLAND, ME)

OYSTER SINGEL

PLUS: RAW OYSTERS WITH OYSTER SINGEL MIGNONETTE · FARMHOUSE
ALE RISOTTO · MOULES À LA BIÈRE · SHANDY ICE POPS

RANGER CREEK
BREWING & DISTILLING
SAN ANTONIO, TX

BREWERY

When we think of Texas we think of barbecue, and lots of it. Slow-cooked brisket ordered fatty with burnt ends, pork ribs gnawed off the bone, and hot sausages that snap when you bite into them. We picture the Lockhart, Texas, institutions Kruez Market, Smitty's, and Black's with their hundred-year-old pits, ban on the usage of forks, and soot-covered walls. We think of smoke, and not just any smoke—mesquite.

And we aren't alone. "Mesquite is what makes Texas barbecue Texas," said Ranger Creek's head brewer, Rob Landerman, when we met up with him at his brewery in San Antonio. Wanting to brew "something that was representative of our state and who we are," Landerman got to work creating a beer that tasted like Texas (and by that we mean mesquite) by combining the German tradition of smoking malt for a classic rauchbier (see Schlenkerla, page 140) with the Texan tradition of building smokers.

Mesquite, a hardy tree that grows rampant in Texas's arid climate, has a nasty habit of sucking up water meant for crops. Farmers hate it. Pit masters love it. And so Ranger Creek is able to trade a local farmer spent grain to use for livestock feed for all the mesquite the brewery could want.

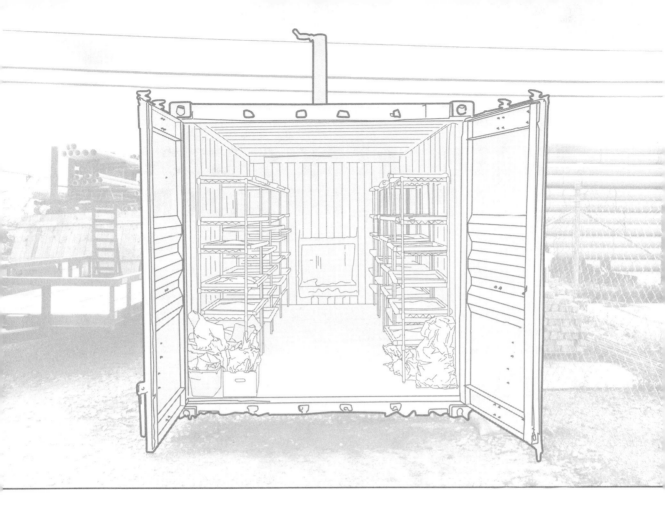

What Ranger Creek does with it is known as cold smoking in the BBQ world. After hand-counting 57 chunks of mesquite, Landerman places the wood in the firebox built into a repurposed 20-foot steel shipping container by a local welder named Rusty Rivets. Donning gas masks, he and two brewers spread out 120 pounds of English Maris Otter malt on handmade screens that sit on wire racks. Once lit, the mesquite burns with a clean, white smoke for an hour, saturating the grain with a rich Texas smokiness.

"IT'S A LOT OF WORK, BUT IT'S A LOT OF FUN TO SMOKE GRAIN," SAID LANDERMAN. IT'S ALSO THE ONLY WAY TO BREW THE PERFECT LONE STAR STATE BARBECUE BEER.

RANGER CREEK'S MESQUITE SMOKED PORTER

6% ABV

PREP

2 coals

5 mesquite briquettes

0.65 lb (294.84 g) Maris Otter malt

60-MINUTE MASH AT 156°F (69°C)

2½ qt (2.37 l) water, plus 1 gal (3.79 l) for sparging

1.25 lb (566.99 g) Maris Otter malt

0.65 lb (294.84 g) mesquite-smoked Maris Otter malt (see prep)

0.25 lb (113.4 g) Caramel 60 malt

0.08 lb (36.29 g) Chocolate malt

0.07 lb (31.75 g) Black malt

*All grains should be milled (see page 15).

60-MINUTE BOIL

0.4 oz (11.34 g) Fuggle hops, divided into thirds

0.2 oz (5.67 g) Tettnang hops

FERMENT

American ale yeast, such as White Labs 001 (see note, page 16)

3 Tbsp (63 g) maple syrup, for bottling

THIS RECIPE COMES COURTESY OF HEAD BREWER ROB LANDERMAN, AND WHILE WE CERTAINLY COULD MAKE THIS BEER WITH SMOKED MALT OFF THE SHELF, IT JUST ISN'T THE SAME. MESQUITE-SMOKED MALT ISN'T SOMETHING YOU CAN BUY. THAT'S WHY THE FOLKS AT RANGER CREEK BUILT THEIR OWN SMOKER AND WHY YOU'LL USE A HOME SMOKER TO DO THE SAME. AND WE PROMISE YOU'LL BE GLAD YOU DID.

PREP In a smoker, light the coals and mesquite briquettes. Let the fire build until the smoke turns white. Smoke 0.65 pound (294.84 grams) Maris Otter malt in a single layer on a wire screen over indirect heat for an hour. Let the malt cure in a closed jar for 5 days before using.

MASH In a medium stockpot, heat 2½ quarts (2.37 liters) water over high heat to 160°F (70°C). Add all the malts and stir gently. The temperature should reduce to 156°F (67°C) within 30 seconds. Turn off the heat. Steep the grains for 60 minutes at 156°F (67°C). Every 10 minutes, stir and take the temperature. If the grains get too cold, turn the heat to high and stir until the temperature returns to 156°C (67°C), then turn off the heat. With 10 minutes left, in a second medium stockpot heat 1 gallon (3.79 liters) water to 170°F (77°C). After the grains have steeped for 60 minutes, turn the heat to high and stir until the temperature reaches 170°F (77°C). Turn off the heat.

SPARGE Place a fine-mesh strainer over a stock-pot and pour the grains into the strainer, reserving the liquid. Pour the 1 gallon (3.79 liters) of 170°F (77°C) water over the grains. Recirculate the collected liquid through the grains once.

BOIL Return the pot with the liquid to the stove and bring to a boil over high heat. When the liquid starts to foam, reduce the heat to a slow rolling boil and add one third of the Fuggle hops. Add the remaining two thirds Fuggle hops after 40 minutes and the Tettnang hops after 55 minutes. Prepare an ice bath by stopping the sink and filling it halfway with water and ice. At the 60-minute mark, turn off the heat. Place the pot in the ice bath and cool to 70°F (21°C), about 30 minutes.

FERMENT Using a funnel and a strainer, pour the liquid into a sanitized fermenter. Add water as needed to fill the jug to the 1-gallon mark. Add the yeast, sanitize your hands, cover the mouth of the jug with one hand, and shake to distribute evenly. Attach a sanitized stopper and tubing to the fermenter and insert the other end of the tubing into a small bowl of sanitizing solution. The solution will begin to bubble as the yeast activates, pushing gas through the tube. Wait 2 to 3 days, until the bubbling has slowed, then replace the tubing system with an airlock. Wait 11 more days, then bottle, using the maple syrup (see page 13 for bottling instructions).

//

SUGGESTED FOOD PAIRINGS Brisket, pork ribs, Kreuz Market's cheddar and jalapeño sausages

NOTE If you prefer not to smoke your own barley, you can use commercially available beechwood or cherrywood smoked malt as an equal substitute.

FOR 5 GALLONS

PREP In a smoker, light the coals and mesquite briquettes. Let the fire build until the smoke turns white. Smoke 3.15 pounds (1428.82 grams) Maris Otter malt in a single layer on a screen over indirect heat for an hour. Let the malt cure in a covered container for 5 days before using.

60-MINUTE MASH AT 156°F (69°C)
3¼ gallons (12.3 liters) water, plus 5 gallons (15.14 liters) for sparging; 6.25 pounds (2834.95 grams) Maris Otter malt; 3.15 pounds (1428.82 grams) mesquite-smoked Maris Otter malt (see prep); 1.25 pounds (566.99 grams) Caramel 60 malt; 0.4 pound (181.44 grams) Chocolate malt; 0.35 pound (158.76 grams) Black malt

60-MINUTE BOIL
2 ounces (56.7 grams) Fuggle hops, divided into thirds; 1 ounce (28.35 grams) Tettnang hops

FERMENT American ale yeast, such as White Labs 001; 1 cup (340 grams) maple syrup, for bottling

LOGSDON ORGANIC
FARMHOUSE ALES

HOOD RIVER, OR

BREWERY

We love a good mystery—especially while on the road. Who doesn't? There's something Carmen Sandiego-esque about seeking answers to important questions that arise in a strange land—in this case, Oregon.

Our quest began shortly after returning from a hop farm 90 minutes east of Portland, where we witnessed the ongoing late-summer harvest with a group of beer writers—grown men and women turned into children by the sight of hops rushing past in every direction on conveyor belts and eventually into massive piles as light and fluffy as a snowdrift atop a black diamond slope. We were in the land of hops, the Pacific Northwest, where nearly 85 percent of all American hops are grown.

And in this land, we weren't expecting an unmarked wax bottle to lead us to a temple of yeast, but if there is such a place in the United States, it's a barn in Hood River where Dave Logsdon and Charles Porter brew traditional Belgian-style farmhouse ales with locally sourced ingredients (which includes cherries from sour cherry trees brought in from Dave's wife's orchard in the Flanders region of Belgium). (If you use liquid yeast when making beer, there's a good chance it came from Wyeast Laboratories, the Oregon-based

yeast manufacturer co-founded by Logsdon in 1986 out of the very barn that's now producing delicate, funky, tart, grassy, farmhouse-style ales.)

Visiting this brewery wasn't in our plan. We were taking the train from Portland to Seattle the next day. Tickets were in hand. It's supposed to be quite the relaxing ride, but we never found out. That's because we found an unmarked, wax-sealed bottle of what we learned the following morning was Logsdon's Seizoen Bretta.

Accidental discoveries like these remind us of our first trip to Europe before we started the Brooklyn Brew Shop, where tomorrow's plans were always a suggestion and the beers always an adventure.

IN THE HEART OF HOP COUNTRY LIES A FARM-HOUSE BREWERY IN THE TRUEST SENSE OF THE TERM.

FARMHOUSE ALE

6% ABV

60-MINUTE MASH AT 152°F (67°C)

2¼ qt (2.12 l) water, plus 1 gal (3.79 l) for sparging

2 lb (907.19 g) Belgian Pilsner malt

0.2 lb (90.72 g) Vienna malt

0.2 lb (90.72 g) Aromatic malt

*All grains should be milled (see page 15).

60-MINUTE BOIL

0.3 oz (8.5 g) East Kent Golding hops, divided into thirds

FERMENT

Wyeast Roeselare Ale Blend (see note, page 16)

3 Tbsp (63 g) honey, for bottling

WE LIKE TO GIVE MULTIPLE YEAST OPTIONS FOR ANY GIVEN BEER RECIPE. EXCEPT FOR THIS ONE, WHERE WE USE A BLEND OF LAMBIC CULTURES FOR SOMETHING THAT TAKES UP TO 18 MONTHS TO FULLY DEVELOP AND CHANGES WITH EVERY PASSING DAY. THE BEER IT CREATES IS BOTH DRY AND REMINISCENT OF SOUR CHERRIES. SINCE THERE ARE ELEMENTS OF WILD YEASTS IN THIS BEER, RIGOROUS SANITIZING BEFORE AND AFTER BREW DAY GETS EXTREMELY IMPORTANT WHEN BREWING.

MASH In a medium stockpot, heat 2¼ quarts (2.12 liters) water over high heat to 160°F (70°C). Add all the malts and stir gently. The temperature should reduce to 150°F (66°C) within 1 minute. Turn off the heat. Steep the grains for 60 minutes between 144°F and 152°F (62°C and 67°C). Every 10 minutes, stir and take the temperature. If the grains get too cold, turn the heat to high and stir until the temperature rises to that range, then turn off the heat. With 10 minutes left, in a second medium stockpot heat 1 gallon (3.79 liters) water to 170°F (77°C). After the grains have steeped for 60 minutes, turn the heat to high and stir until the temperature reaches 170°F (77°C). Turn off the heat.

SPARGE Place a fine-mesh strainer over a stockpot and pour the grains into the strainer, reserving the liquid. Pour the 1 gallon (3.79 liters) of 170°F (77°C) water over the grains. Recirculate the collected liquid through the grains once.

BOIL Return the pot with the liquid to the stove and bring to a boil over high heat. When the liquid starts to foam, reduce the heat to a slow rolling boil and add one third of the East Kent Golding hops. Add the remaining two thirds hops after 50 minutes. Prepare an ice bath by stopping the sink and filling it halfway with water and ice. At the 60-minute mark, turn off the heat. Place the pot in the ice bath and cool to 70°F (21°C), about 30 minutes.

FERMENT Using a funnel and a strainer, pour the liquid into a sanitized fermenter. Add water as needed to fill the jug to the 1-gallon mark. Add the yeast, sanitize your hands, cover the mouth of the jug with one hand, and shake to distribute evenly. Attach a sanitized stopper and tubing to the fermenter and insert the other end of the tubing into a small bowl of sanitizing solution. The solution will begin to bubble as the yeast activates, pushing gas through the tube. Wait 2 to 3 days, until the bubbling has slowed, then replace the tubing system with an airlock. Wait 11 more days, then bottle, using the honey (see page 13 for bottling instructions).

SUGGESTED FOOD PAIRINGS Radishes with salted butter, rack of lamb, strawberry-rhubarb pie

FOR 5 GALLONS

60-MINUTE MASH AT 152°F (67°C)
2¾ gallons (10.41 liters) water, plus 5 gallons (18.93 liters) for sparging; 10 pounds (4535.92 grams) Belgian Pilsner malt; 1 pound (453.59 grams) Vienna malt; 1 pound (453.59 grams) Aromatic malt

60-MINUTE BOIL 1.5 ounces (42.52 grams) East Kent Golding hops, divided into thirds

FERMENT Wyeast Roeselare Ale Blend; 1 cup (340 grams) honey, for bottling

BIRRIFICIO MONTEGIOCO

PIEDMONT, ITALY

BREWERY

Quatra Runa, one of our favorite beers in the world, is brewed by three men in an old granary tucked away in the hills of northern Italy. Each bottle is filled and individually wrapped in paper by hand before going out the door. But before that, the beer is blended with a sweet and pulpy wild-fermented juice made from local peaches aged for three years in one of just seven oak barrels.

It's no coincidence that we found ourselves and this beer (Quatra Runa) in Piedmont, the home and birthplace of the international Slow Food movement. Imagine surrounding yourself with some of the most amazing ingredients in the world. Juicy low-hanging pears, peaches, and citrus line the sides of steeply winding trails.

"This is my home," said head brewer Riccardo Franzosi. "When I'm more than ten kilometers from here, I feel strange." We immediately understood what he meant, and even if we hadn't, he and the two other brewers (one of whom learned English from watching David Letterman) made sure we did. For lunch, Riccardo sliced salami that had cured with their beer and was made from pigs raised down the road on spent grain from their brewery.

When Italy comes to mind, beer doesn't. When we brought this up to Riccardo, we quickly realized the error in our thought process. "I have a lot of friends that make very good wine in this area," he said, and with the goal being enjoyment rather than competition, he thought making beer was a better idea.

It seemed obvious after hearing this (if not tasting the beer). If something is good, then it's good. Sitting around the lunch table, there were no wine people or beer people. We don't have chicken people or beef people. If something is made with care, a respect for craft, and the freshest ingredients possible, then it's just good, and something to be appreciated.

"THIS IS MY HOME. WHEN I'M MORE THAN TEN KILOMETERS FROM HERE, I FEEL STRANGE."

—RICCARDO FRANZOSI,
HEAD BREWER

BLENDED FRUIT BEER

6.5% ABV

PREP

2 ripe stone fruits, pitted and peeled

60-MINUTE MASH AT 152°F (67°C)

2½ qt (2.37 l) water, plus 1 gal (3.79 l) for sparging

1.5 lb (680.39 g) Belgian Pilsner malt

0.3 lb (136.08 g) Belgian Biscuit malt

0.2 lb (90.72 g) Caramel 10 malt

0.1 lb (45.36 g) Belgian Munich malt

0.1 lb (45.36 g) torrified wheat

*All grains should be milled (see page 15).

60-MINUTE BOIL

0.3 oz (8.5 g) Styrian Golding hops, divided into thirds

FERMENT

Belgian ale yeast, such as Safale S-33 (see note, page 16)

3 Tbsp (63 g) honey, for bottling

WHILE WE USUALLY MAKE BEERS WE CAN DRINK IN A MONTH, WE APPRECIATE ONES THAT CANNOT BE MADE BY IMPATIENT PEOPLE. BREWING WITH FRUITS AND WILD YEASTS CAN TAKE LONGER TO FULLY DEVELOP INTO A DELICATE AND COMPLEX FINISHED PRODUCT. THIS BEER HAS US SCOURING THE FARMER'S MARKETS BACK IN BROOKLYN FOR THE FRESHEST FRUITS WE CAN FIND. THE FRUITS WE USE CHANGE DEPENDING ON THE SEASON, FROM PEACHES AND PLUMS TO APPLES AND QUINCE.

//

PREP In a blender, blend the fruit until smooth. Pour into a sanitized fermenter and let sit for 1 week.

MASH In a medium stockpot, heat 2½ quarts (2.37 liters) water over high heat to 160°F (70°C). Add all the malts and stir gently. The temperature should reduce to 150°F (66°C) within 1 minute. Turn off the heat. Steep the grains for 60 minutes between 144°F and 152°F (62°C and 67°C). Every 10 minutes, stir and take the temperature. If the grains get too cold, turn the heat to high and stir until the temperature rises to that range, then turn off the heat. With 10 minutes left, in a second medium stockpot heat 1 gallon (3.79 liters) water to 170°F (77°C). After the grains have steeped for 60 minutes, turn the heat to high and stir until the temperature reaches 170°F (77°C). Turn off the heat.

SPARGE Place a fine-mesh strainer over a stockpot, and pour the grains into the strainer, reserving the liquid. Pour the 1 gallon (3.79 liters) of 170°F (77°C) water over the grains. Recirculate the collected liquid through the grains once.

BOIL Return the pot with the liquid to the stove and bring to a boil over high heat. When the liquid starts to foam, reduce the heat to a slow rolling boil and add one third of the Styrian Golding hops. Add another third of the hops after 30 minutes and the final third after 45 minutes. Prepare an ice bath by stopping the sink and filling it halfway with water and ice. At the 60-minute mark, turn off the heat. Place the pot in the ice bath and cool to 70°F (21°C), about 30 minutes.

FERMENT Using a funnel and a strainer, pour the liquid into the fermenter with the fermented stone fruit juice. Add water as needed to fill the jug to the 1-gallon mark. Add the yeast, sanitize your hands, cover the mouth of the jug with one hand, and shake to distribute evenly. Attach a sanitized stopper and tubing to the fermenter and insert the other end of the tubing into a small bowl of sanitizing solution. The solution will begin to bubble as the yeast activates, pushing gas through the tube. Wait 2 to 3 days, until the bubbling has slowed, then replace the tubing system with an airlock. Wait 11 more days, then siphon the beer to a second fermentation jug. Let ferment for 3 more months. When the surface area is free of any bubbles, bottle using the honey (see page 13 for bottling instructions) in Belgian-style bottles (see note, page 15).

//

SUGGESTED FOOD PAIRINGS Focaccia, salumi, shaved truffles

FOR 5 GALLONS

PREP 10 ripe stone fruits, pitted and peeled

60-MINUTE MASH AT 152°F (67°C)
3¼ gallons (12.3 liters) water, plus 4 gallons (15.14 liters) for sparging; 7.5 pounds (3401.94 grams) Belgian Pilsner malt; 1.5 pounds (680.38 grams) Belgian Biscuit malt; 1 pound (453.59 grams) Caramel 10 malt; 0.5 pound (226.8 grams) Belgian Munich malt; 0.5 pound (226.8 grams) torrified wheat

60-MINUTE BOIL 1.5 ounces (42.52 grams) Styrian Golding hops, divided into thirds

FERMENT Belgian ale yeast, such as Safale S-33; 1 cup (340 grams) honey, for bottling

BREWERY OMMEGANG

COOPERSTOWN, NY

We have a warm spot reserved in our hearts for visiting farms. Stepping down from our big white pickup truck (normally employed for lugging beer kits to the Brooklyn Flea) into a fog-blanketed puddle of mud at the crack of dawn reminds us of the homesteading lives we never lived. The site now occupied by Brewery Ommegang was once a farm, but not of the poultry, pig, and cattle kind. It was a hop farm in the middle of upstate New York, which, prior to Prohibition, two world wars, and a blight, was the top hop-producing region in the United States, and Cooperstown was its center.

In the years since, hop production has moved westward to Oregon and Washington, but in 1997 Ommegang opened its doors and its fermenters to bring a bit of beer back to a city better known for baseball.

We try to make it up to Ommegang at least once a year, ideally for the Belgium Comes to Cooperstown festival, where breweries from around the world gather to pour Belgian-style ales for drinkers who hail from near and far. While we're of the mind that beer festivals might not be the best place to thoughtfully taste and retain information on new beers (or much of anything in more extreme cases where large servings are plentiful), BCTC makes up for it by asking you to pitch a tent on the brewery's bucolic surroundings and stay the night.

Tent cities mirroring actual cities pop up once the official daytime event concludes so that the unofficial fest can begin. Beer in hand, wandering from New York to Philadelphia takes only minutes. Legs of prosciutto are sliced in one city while homemade sausage is grilled just a few feet away in another.

In the morning, dew covers everything. Cities disperse, tents fold up, grills are packed away. Cars drive in opposite directions until next year, when everyone comes together once more for a beer.

WHEN HEADING TO BELGIAN COMES TO COOPERSTOWN, MAKE SURE TO BRING FOOD, LOTS OF WATER, AND BEER-LOVING FRIENDS YOU DON'T MIND SLEEPING NEXT TO.

IPA, BELGIAN STYLE

6.5% ABV

60-MINUTE MASH AT 152°F (67°C)

2½ qt (2.37 l) water, plus 1 gal (3.79 l) for sparging

2 lb (907.19 g) Belgian Pilsner malt

0.4 lb (181.44 g) Munich malt

0.15 lb (68.04 g) Caramel 10 malt

*All grains should be milled (see page 15).

60-MINUTE BOIL

0.1 oz (2.83 g) Chinook hops

0.1 oz (2.83 g) Centennial hops

0.3 oz (8.5 g) Simcoe hops, divided into thirds

FERMENT

Belgian ale yeast, such as Safale S-33 (see note, page 16)

3 Tbsp (63 g) honey, for bottling

IPAS AND BELGIAN-STYLE ALES MAY SEEM LIKE THEY'RE ON THE OPPOSITE ENDS OF THE BEER SPECTRUM. IF SUCH A SPECTRUM COULD EVER EXIST, IT WOULD PROBABLY PLACE IPAS ON THE BITTER END AND BELGIAN ALES ON THE SWEET END. BUT IT'S SAFE TO SAY BEER TASTES AND STYLES AREN'T ACTUALLY THIS SIMPLE. FOR THIS RECIPE, WE MERGED THE HOP AROMAS OF AMERICAN IPAS BURSTING WITH CITRUS AND PINE WITH THE PLEASANT MALT AND YEAST CHARACTER OF BELGIAN-STYLE ALES FOR A BEER THAT TRANSCENDS STYLES AND CROSSES OCEANS.

MASH In a medium stockpot, heat 2½ quarts (2.37 liters) water over high heat to 160°F (70°C). Add all the malts and stir gently. The temperature should reduce to 150°F (66°C) within 1 minute. Turn off the heat. Steep the grains for 60 minutes between 144°F and 152°F (62°C and 67°C). Every 10 minutes, stir and take the temperature. If the grains get too cold, turn the heat to high and stir until the temperature rises to that range, then turn off the heat. With 10 minutes left, in a second medium stockpot heat 1 gallon (3.79 liters) water to 170°F (77°C). After the grains have steeped for 60 minutes, turn the heat to high and stir until the temperature reaches 170°F (77°C). Turn off the heat.

SPARGE Place a fine-mesh strainer over a stockpot and pour the grains into the strainer, reserving the liquid. Pour the 1 gallon (3.79 liters) of 170°F (77°C) water over the grains. Recirculate the collected liquid through the grains once.

BOIL Return the pot with the liquid to the stove and bring to a boil over high heat. When the liquid starts to foam, reduce the heat to a slow rolling boil and add the Chinook hops. Add the Centennial hops after 30 minutes. Add one third of the Simcoe hops after 50 minutes. Prepare an ice bath by stopping the sink and filling it halfway with water and ice. At the 60-minute mark, turn off the heat, add another third of the Simcoe hops (reserving the final third for dry-hopping during fermentation). Place the pot in the ice bath and cool to 70°F (21°C), about 30 minutes.

FERMENT Using a funnel and a strainer, pour the liquid into a sanitized fermenter. Add water as needed to fill the jug to the 1-gallon mark. Add the yeast, sanitize your hands, cover the mouth of the jug with one hand, and shake to distribute evenly. Attach a sanitized stopper and tubing to the fermenter and insert the other end of the tubing into a small bowl of sanitizing solution. The solution will begin to bubble as the yeast activates, pushing gas through the tube. Wait 2 to 3 days, until the bubbling has slowed, then add the remaining one third Simcoe hops directly into the fermenter and replace the tubing system with an airlock. Wait 11 more days, then bottle, using the honey (see page 13 for bottling instructions).

//

SUGGESTED FOOD PAIRINGS English cheddar grilled cheese sandwich, foie gras on toast, country ham

FOR 5 GALLONS
60-MINUTE MASH AT 152°F (67°C)
3¼ gallons (12.3 liters) water, plus 4 gallons (15.14 liters) for sparging; 10 pounds (4535.92 grams) Belgian Pilsner malt; 2 pounds (907.19 grams) Munich malt; 0.75 pound (340.19 grams) Caramel 10 malt

60-MINUTE BOIL
0.5 ounce (14.17 grams) Chinook hops; 0.5 ounce (14.17 grams) Centennial hops; 1.5 ounces (42.52 grams) Simcoe hops, divided into thirds

FERMENT Belgian ale yeast, such as Safale S-33; 1 cup (340 grams) honey, for bottling

CIGAR CITY BREWING

TAMPA, FL

BREWERY

With more than 400 beers under their belts (in just four years) and continuing expansion, Cigar City Brewing in Tampa has scaled back out-of-state distribution and amped up production in an effort to serve its (kind of enormous) home state.

"Florida is a really big state. It's almost like we're three states," Cigar City's vice president Justin Clark informs us. "You can drive from Key West for 12 hours and still be in Florida."

Serving their state is exactly what they were thinking when Cigar City brewers switched over the majority of their beers from bottles to cans this year. It made sense for their location, where beers are often enjoyed on the golf course and poolside; for their beer's freshness (Florida's strong rays can damage hoppy beers); and for their community, which plays host to a Ball factory churning out eight million cans a day.

And it's their community that gathers around their tasting room—complete with a man hand-rolling cigars—trying flights of their newest, oddest (they made a beer brewed in part with puddle water from a skatepark that was aged on skateboard decks), and favorite brews.

It takes a lot of new ideas to brew up a hundred-plus beers per year. Ideas go from "that's the stupidest idea I've ever heard" to "we'll try it," resulting in one-off test batches to tasting room mainstays to full-scale production runs to be enjoyed across Florida. "Working here, everyone is really encouraged to be creative," Clark added, "which keeps us all entertained and wanting to be here."

He says that even after scaling back geographically, "We are constantly increasing production and in a state of expansion." In the world of Cigar City, that means not only more finished cans and kegs rolling off the production line, but more styles of beer and an expansion of what a beer can be.

IF YOU FLY INTO TAMPA INTERNATIONAL AIRPORT, STOP BY CIGAR CITY'S 3.5 BARREL BREWPUB FOR AN AIRPORT EXCLUSIVE TONY JANNUS PALE ALE.

CUCUMBER SAISON

6% ABV

60-MINUTE MASH AT 152°F (67°C)

2½ qt (2.37 l) water, plus 1 gal (3.79 l) for sparging

2 lb (907.19 g) Belgian Pilsner malt

0.2 lb (90.72 g) Caramel 10 malt

0.15 lb (68.04 g) Aromatic malt

*All grains should be milled (see page 15).

60-MINUTE BOIL

0.4 oz (11.34 g) Hallertau hops, divided into quarters

0.1 oz (2.83 g) Spaltz hops

FERMENT

1 large seedless cucumber, washed, halved, and thinly sliced

Belgian ale yeast, such as Safale S-33 (see note, page 16)

3 Tbsp (63 g) honey, for bottling

THE IDEA FOR A CUCUMBER BEER WAS ONE THAT CLARK CAME UP WITH AFTER HAVING A CUCUMBER GIMLET AND WANTING TO BRING THAT REFRESHMENT INTO A BEER. AND IT WAS ONE OF THE FEW IDEAS THAT STEPHEN FELT TOTALLY SCOOPED ON, AS HE HAD BEEN TALKING ABOUT INCORPORATING CUCUMBER INTO A BEER QUITE A BIT.

WHEN WE MET UP WITH CLARK WE HAD ONLY ONE THING TO SAY TO HIM—THAT HIS CUCUMBER SAISON TOTALLY BEAT US TO THE PUNCH. TO WHICH HIS RESPONSE WAS, "RIGHT ON. WELL, YOU GUYS SHOULD STILL MAKE ONE, TOO." SO WE DID. WITH A NOD TO CIGAR CITY, OF COURSE.

///

MASH In a medium stockpot, heat 2½ quarts (2.37 liters) water over high heat to 160°F (70°C). Add all the malts and stir gently. The temperature should reduce to 150°F (66°C) within 1 minute. Turn off the heat. Steep the grains for 60 minutes between 144°F and 152°F (62°C and 67°C). Every 10 minutes, stir and take the temperature. If the grains get too cold, turn the heat to high and stir until the temperature rises to that range, then turn off the heat. With 10 minutes left, in a second medium stockpot heat 1 gallon (3.79 liters) water to 170°F (77°C). After the grains have steeped for 60 minutes, turn the heat to high and stir until the temperature reaches 170°F (77°C). Turn off the heat.

SPARGE Place a fine-mesh strainer over a stock-pot and pour the grains into the strainer, reserving the liquid. Pour the 1 gallon (3.79 liters) of 170°F (77°C) water over the grains. Recirculate the collected liquid through the grains once.

BOIL Return the pot with the liquid to the stove and bring to a boil over high heat. When the liquid starts to foam, reduce the heat to a slow rolling boil. Add half of the Hallertau hops after 15 minutes. Add one quarter of the Hallertau hops after 40 minutes and the remainder after 50 minutes. Prepare an ice bath by stopping the sink and filling it halfway with water and ice. At the 60-minute mark, turn off the heat and add the Spaltz hops. Place the pot in the ice bath and cool to 70°F (21°C), about 30 minutes.

FERMENT Using a funnel and a strainer, pour the liquid into a sanitized fermenter. Add water as needed to fill the jug to the 1-gallon mark. Add the yeast, sanitize your hands, cover the mouth of the jug with one hand, and shake to distribute evenly. Add the sliced cucumber directly to the fermenter. Attach a sanitized stopper and tubing to the fermenter and insert the other end of the tubing into a small bowl of sanitizing solution. The solution will begin to bubble as the yeast activates, pushing gas through the tube. Wait 2 to 3 days, until the bubbling has slowed, then replace the tubing system with an airlock. Wait 11 more days, then bottle, using the honey (see page 13 for bottling instructions).

//

SUGGESTED FOOD PAIRINGS Lamb burgers, tzatziki, shepherd's salad

FOR 5 GALLONS
60-MINUTE MASH AT 152°F (67°C)
3¼ gallons (12.3 liters) water, plus 4 gallons (15.14 liters) for sparging; 10 pounds (4535.92 grams) Belgian Pilsner malt; 1 pound (453.59 grams) Caramel 10 malt; 0.75 pound (340.19 grams) Aromatic malt

60-MINUTE BOIL
2 ounces (56.7 grams) Hallertau hops, divided into quarters; 0.5 ounce (14.17 grams) Spaltz hops

FERMENT
5 large seedless cucumbers, washed, halved, and thinly sliced; Belgian ale yeast, such as Safale S-33; 1 cup (340 grams) honey, for bottling

JESTER KING

AUSTIN, TX

BREWERY

Do-it-yourself, or DIY for short, is a popular phrase. Making beer is DIY. So is making pasta or yogurt. Fixing a car or building a computer is, too. Doing something yourself—made by you and for you—always feels good.

Since we can't think of anything more DIY than building yourself a 30-barrel brewhouse, we visited Jester King in Austin, Texas, to see how a lonely field in hill country becomes a brewery.

"This was an old machine shop we found in southern Texas. We went down there, took the building apart, and built it back together in hill country," says brewery co-founder Jeff Stuffings.

Knowing they put up the corrugated steel walls, laid down the roof, filled in the insulation, and wired the building's electricity (after reading up on circuits at the library) nearly excuses the fact that they were missing one of their four walls at the time of our visit. "It gives it a farmhouse feel," says Stuffings.

Building a brewery, however, proved to be the easiest part of making (and selling) beer in Texas, where beer labeling laws often require styles to be mislabeled because the classifications used are based on alcohol

percentages instead of actual stylistic differences. This often results in lagers being called ales and really nice farmhouse beers like the kinds Jester King specializes in being classified as malt liquors.

Since its inception, Jester King has been hard at work trying to push legislative changes that would benefit the Lone Star State's beer-drinking population, but it's been an uphill battle—one that makes raising a barn or a brewery seem easy.

THERE'S NO SHORTAGE OF BBQ PIT STOPS ON THE WAY FROM DOWN-TOWN AUSTIN TO THE JESTER KING.

TABLE BEER

4.2% ABV

60-MINUTE MASH AT 152°F (67°C)

1½ qt (1.42 l) water, plus 1¼ gal (4.73 l) for sparging

0.95 lb (430.91 g) Maris Otter malt

0.1 lb (45.36 g) flaked oats

0.05 lb (22.68 g) Cara-Pils malt

*All grains should be milled (see page 15).

60-MINUTE BOIL

0.36 oz (10.2 g) Citra hops, divided into quarters

FERMENT

Belgian ale yeast, such as Safale S-33 (see note, page 16)

3 Tbsp (63 g) honey, for bottling

SUMMER IN HILL COUNTRY IS NOT LIKE SUMMER IN BROOKLYN. IN NEW YORK, IT GETS HOT, STICKY, AND UNCOMFORTABLE, BUT IN TEXAS, SUMMER DAYS IN THE SUN FEEL LIKE THE INSIDE OF AN OVEN. THANKFULLY, BREWERS BEGAN A TRADITION OF HELPING PEOPLE LONG BEFORE AIR-CONDITIONING CAME AROUND. MUCH AS THE LIGHT, EASY-DRINKING WINES OF SOUTHERN ITALY MAINTAIN A CONSTANT SPOT ON THE TABLE THROUGHOUT LONG SUMMER DAYS AND NIGHTS, LOW-ALCOHOL BELGIAN-STYLE TABLE BEERS, LIKE JESTER KING'S LE PETIT PRINCE, HAVE LONG ACCOMPANIED THE SUN'S MORE ACTIVE SEASONS AND ARE PERFECT FOR THE TEXAS HEAT.

//

MASH In a medium stockpot, heat 1½ quarts (1.42 liters) water over high heat to 160°F (70°C). Add all the malts and stir gently. The temperature should reduce to 150°F (66°C) within 1 minute. Turn off the heat. Steep the grains for 60 minutes between 144°F and 152°F (62°C and 67°C). Every 10 minutes, stir and take the temperature. If the grains get too cold, turn the heat to high and stir until the temperature rises to that range, then turn off the heat. With 10 minutes left, in a second medium stockpot heat 1¼ gallons (4.73 liters) water to 170°F (77°C). After the grains have steeped for 60 minutes, turn the heat to high and stir until the temperature reaches 170°F (77°C). Turn off the heat.

SPARGE Place a fine-mesh strainer over a stock-pot and pour the grains into the strainer, reserving the liquid. Pour the 1¼ gallons (4.73 liters) of 170°F (77°C) water over the grains. Recirculate the collected liquid through the grains once.

BOIL Return the pot with the liquid to the stove and bring to a boil over high heat. When the liquid starts to foam, reduce the heat to a slow rolling boil and add one quarter of the Citra hops. Add another quarter of the Citra hops after 45 minutes. Prepare an ice bath by stopping the sink and filling it halfway with water and ice. At the 60-minute mark, turn off the heat, add one quarter of the Citra hops (reserving the final quarter for dry-hopping during fermentation). Place the pot in the ice bath and cool to 70°F (21°C), about 30 minutes.

FERMENT Using a funnel and a strainer, pour the liquid into a sanitized fermenter. Add water as needed to fill the jug to the 1-gallon mark. Add the yeast, sanitize your hands, cover the mouth of the jug with one hand, and shake to distribute evenly. Attach a sanitized stopper and tubing to the fermenter and insert the other end of the tubing into a small bowl of sanitizing solution. The solution will begin to bubble as the yeast activates, pushing gas through the tube. Wait 2 to 3 days, until the bubbling has slowed, then add the remaining quarter Citra hops directly to the fermenter and replace the tubing system with an airlock. Wait 11 more days, then bottle, using the honey (see page 13 for bottling instructions).

//

SUGGESTED FOOD PAIRINGS Chopped salad, burgers, quail

FOR 5 GALLONS
60-MINUTE MASH AT 152°F (67°C)
2 gallons (7.57 liters) water, plus 5 gallons (18.93 liters) for sparging; 4.75 pounds (2154.56 grams) Maris Otter malt; 0.5 pound (226.8 grams) flaked oats; 0.25 pound (113.4 grams) Cara-Pils malt

60-MINUTE BOIL 1.8 ounces (51 grams) Citra hops, divided into quarters

FERMENT Belgian ale yeast, such as Safale S-33; 1 cup (340 grams) honey, for bottling

WICKED WEED

BREWERY

ASHEVILLE, NC

We've been to breweries held together by duct tape and filled with mismatched fermenters bought piece by piece as the brewery grew. We've seen our fair share of improvised augers, converted dairy equipment, and bottling lines rigged with extra-long conveyor belts to account for how often the machine would malfunction.

So when we headed to the one-month-old Wicked Weed in Asheville, North Carolina, we expected to see an oversized pilot system, undersized staff, and a fair amount of tape. What we didn't expect was a pristine, multilevel, full-scale restaurant and brewhouse that opened with 17 beers on tap.

Wicked Weed's goal is to keep changing those taps and trying out new recipes. "At least one out of every three or four brews is a new beer for us," says co-founder and brewer Walt Dickinson.

Running with the story that King Henry VIII proclaimed hops to be a "wicked and pernicious weed" and forbade their use in the English ales of the early 1500s, Dickinson added, "We wanted to brew hop-forward beers that paid homage to traditional, old-world brewing methods like barrel aging and open fermentation." What they have built is a system designed to have the versatility to produce different styles of beer (and the prettiest sterile room, with an open-air fermenter enclosed in glass, that we've ever come across).

The resulting beers bounce between West Coast–style aromatic IPAs and Belgian-style ales brewed with ingredients both local (sweet potatoes, grits) and not-so-local (passion fruit, mangos). They also use the same base grains in their saison series and change the fruit, vegetables, herbs, and spices for a myriad of effects. The chalkboard of what's on draft is constantly changing depending on the brewers' whims and what's in season.

To Dickinson the goal is simple: "How do we make enough beer to keep everybody's pint glass full and keep our board looking like this?"

"HOPS ARE A WICKED AND PERNICIOUS WEED."

—KING HENRY VIII

STRAWBERRY RHUBARB STRONG ALE

7.7% ABV

60-MINUTE MASH AT 152°F (67°C)

2½ qt (2.37 l) water, plus 1 gal (3.79 l) for sparging

2.3 lb (1043.26 g) Belgian Pilsner malt

0.15 lb (68.04 g) Belgian Biscuit malt

*All grains should be milled (see page 15).

60-MINUTE BOIL

0.1 oz (2.83 g) Challenger hops

2 rhubarb stalks (120 g), cut into 3-inch (7.6-centimeter) pieces

0.2 oz (5.67 g) Cluster hops, divided in half

16 strawberries, hulled and quartered

0.3 lb (136.08 g) Belgian Candi Sugar

FERMENT

Belgian ale yeast, such as Safale S-33 (see note, page 16)

3 Tbsp (63 g) honey, for bottling

SOME BEERS YOU DRINK. OTHERS YOU EAT. THIS IS THE LATTER. NOT TO SAY IT'S THICK, HEAVY, AND SYRUPY. IT'S QUITE THE OPPOSITE: LIGHT IN BODY AND GOES DOWN EASY. IT'S A HIGH-ALCOHOL TASTE OF SUMMER WHOSE PILLOWY HEAD CONSISTS OF BUBBLES POPPING WITH PLUMES OF STRAWBERRY THAT FILL YOUR NOSE WITH EVERY SIP. THE RHUBARB (NOT THE SWEETEST OF SUMMER FARE) HELPS TO ADD BALANCE AND A LITTLE TARTNESS. DRINK THIS FRESH (PREFERABLY OUTDOORS UNDER A SHADY TREE) OR AGE IT FOR A COUPLE OF EXTRA MONTHS TO MELLOW OUT THE ALCOHOL.

//

MASH In a medium stockpot, heat 2½ quarts (2.37 liters) water over high heat to 160°F (70°C). Add all the malts and stir gently. The temperature should reduce to 150°F (66°C) within 1 minute. Turn off the heat. Steep the grains for 60 minutes between 144°F and 152°F (62°C and 67°C). Every 10 minutes, stir and take the temperature. If the grains get too cold, turn the heat to high and stir until the temperature rises to that range, then turn off the heat. With 10 minutes left, in a second medium stockpot heat 1 gallon (3.79 liters) water to 170°F (77°C). After the grains have steeped for 60 minutes, turn the heat to high and stir until the temperature reaches 170°F (77°C). Turn off the heat.

SPARGE Place a fine-mesh strainer over a stock-pot and pour the grains into the strainer, reserving the liquid. Pour the 1 gallon (3.79 liters) of 170°F (77°C) water over the grains. Recirculate the collected liquid through the grains once.

BOIL Return the pot with the liquid to the stove and bring to a boil over high heat. When the liquid starts to foam, reduce the heat to a slow rolling boil and add the Challenger hops. Add the rhubarb and half of the Cluster hops after 30 minutes. Add the remaining Cluster hops after 55 minutes. Prepare an ice bath by stopping the sink and filling it halfway with water and ice. At the 60-minute mark, turn off the heat, add the strawberries and Belgian Candi Sugar, and stir to dissolve the sugar. Place the pot in the ice bath and cool to 70°F (21°C), about 30 minutes.

FERMENT Using a funnel and a strainer, pour the liquid into a sanitized fermenter. Add water as needed to fill the jug to the 1-gallon mark. Add the yeast, sanitize your hands, cover the mouth of the jug with one hand, and shake to distribute evenly. Attach a sanitized stopper and tubing to the fermenter and insert the other end of the tubing into a small bowl of sanitizing solution. The solution will begin to bubble as the yeast activates, pushing gas through the tube. Wait 2 to 3 days, until the bubbling has slowed, then replace the tubing

system with an airlock. Wait 11 more days, then bottle, using the honey (see page 13 for bottling instructions).

//

SUGGESTED FOOD PAIRINGS Strawberry-rhubarb pie, freshly whipped cream, summer squash soup

FOR 5 GALLONS
60-MINUTE MASH AT 152°F (67°C)
3¼ gallons (12.3 liters) of water, plus 4 gallons (15.14 liters) for sparging; 11.5 pounds (5216.31 grams) Belgian Pilsner malt; 0.75 pound (340.19 grams) Belgian Biscuit malt

60-MINUTE BOIL 0.5 ounce (14.17 grams) Challenger hops; 10 rhubarb stalks (600 grams), cut into 3-inch (7.6-centimeter) pieces; 1 ounce (28.35 grams) Cluster hops, divided in half; 5 pints (1275.73 grams) strawberries, hulled and quartered; 1.5 pounds (680.39 grams) Belgian Candi Sugar

FERMENT Belgian ale yeast, such as Safale S-33; 1 cup (340 grams) honey, for bottling

BUNKER BREWING

PORTLAND, ME

BREWERY

We've all been the recipients of a hand-me-down at some point, be it the just-a-little-too-big winter coat or the not-quite-long-enough-sleeves suit jacket. Some day long in the future we plan on being the recipients of cribs, strollers, and whatever else it takes to raise a little human. And when that person grows up, he or she will inherit the things we no longer need but don't want to throw out.

Breweries too have a rich, interconnected hand-me-down circle of used equipment that helps make new breweries possible and small breweries grow without breaking the bank (at least not too badly). A 10-barrel brewhouse might have been fine for pouring pints in the taproom and at a few local bars, but 30 barrels may just be the key to statewide domination (or so a brewery with expansion on its mind might hope).

Co-owner and brewer Chresten Sorensen at Bunker Brewing showed us his secondhand three-and-a-half barrel system, common in a one- or two-man show, in between pouring beers for a bridal party that was drinking outside the one-room brewery. To be shown around this size brewery is to simply turn around. The office is lofted, and the storage is wherever possible.

The mash tuns and fermenters, purchased from Maine Beer Company just a few miles outside Portland, are small and manageable but require long days or multiple batches to supply a city thirsty for beer.

This is the second used brew system that Bunker has added at the brewery. And as demand grows, it likely won't be their last. Whether or not the next one also comes from Maine Beer or from a few states away, one thing that's up in the air is what upstart brewer will be the proud owner of pieces of Bunker's brewhouse in a few years.

But for now, this two-man show turns out a rotating list of beers to serve at the brewery as well as a rapidly expanding list of local bars and restaurants.

PICK UP A SHOT OF ESPRESSO AND A BAG OF COFFEE BEANS AT TANDEM COFFEE NEXT DOOR.

OYSTER SINGEL

4.3% ABV

60-MINUTE MASH AT 152°F (67°C)

2 qt (1.89 l) water, plus 1.2 gal (4.54 l) for sparging

1.5 lb (680.39 g) Belgian Pilsner malt

0.2 lb (90.72 g) Cara-Pils malt

*All grains should be milled (see page 15).

60-MINUTE BOIL

0.1 oz (2.83 g) Sorachi Ace hops

3 fresh oysters in the shell, rinsed

0.2 oz (5.67 g) Saaz hops

0.1 oz (2.83 g) Spaltz hops

FERMENT

Belgian ale yeast, such as Safbrew T-58 (see note, page 16)

3 Tbsp (63 g) honey, for bottling

IT SEEMS STRANGE TO SOME PEOPLE THAT WE MIGHT DRIVE 12 HOURS FOR BEER AND OYSTERS, BUT THEY'RE TWO OF OUR FAVORITE FOODS, ESPECIALLY WHEN THE RIGHT BEER IS PAIRED WITH AN OYSTER FRESH FROM THE OCEAN. A PERFECT OYSTER SHOULD TASTE LIKE THE WATER FROM WHICH IT WAS PLUCKED. IT'S LIGHT ON THE PALATE AND WELCOMING OF A BEVERAGE TO WASH IT DOWN. BUT NOT JUST ANY BEER WILL DO—WE SPRING FOR ONE THAT'S DRY, EASY-DRINKING, EFFER-VESCENT, AND A LITTLE SPICY. SINGELS ARE THE LITTLEST SIBLINGS TO BELGIAN DUBBELS AND TRIPELS. THEY'RE LOW IN ALCOHOL, MEANT TO BE CONSUMED WITH FOOD, AND GIVE US A GREAT BASE TO TRULY COMBINE OUR LOVE FOR BREWING WITH OUR LOVE FOR EATING OYSTERS. THE ADDITION OF OYS-TERS TO BEER HAS TRADITIONALLY BEEN LIMITED TO OYSTER STOUTS. ADDING OYSTERS TO THE BOIL OF A SINGEL GIVES IT A MINERALITY AND HINT OF BRININESS THAT MAKES IT THE PERFECT FRIEND OF FINDS ON THE HALF-SHELL.

MASH In a medium stockpot, heat 2 quarts (1.89 liters) water over high heat to 160°F (70°C). Add all the malts and stir gently. The temperature should reduce to 150°F (66°C) within 1 minute. Turn off the heat. Steep the grains for 60 minutes between 144°F and 152°F (62°C and 67°C). Every 10 minutes, stir and take the temperature. If the grains get too cold, turn the heat to high and stir until the temperature rises to that range, then turn off the heat. With 10 minutes left, in a second medium stockpot heat 1.2 gallons (4.54 liters) water to 170°F (77°C). After the grains have steeped for 60 minutes, turn the heat to high and stir until the temperature reaches 170°F (77°C). Turn off the heat.

SPARGE Place a fine-mesh strainer over a stock-pot and pour the grains into the strainer, reserving the liquid. Pour the 1.2 gallons (4.54 liters) of 170°F (77°C) water over the grains. Recirculate the collected liquid through the grains once.

BOIL Return the pot with the liquid to the stove and bring to a boil over high heat. When the liquid starts to foam, reduce the heat to a slow rolling boil. Add the Sorachi Ace hops and oysters (in the shell) after 30 minutes. Add the Saaz hops after 50 minutes. Prepare an ice bath by stopping the sink and filling it halfway with water and ice. At the 60-minute mark, turn off the heat and add the Spaltz hops. Place the pot in the ice bath and cool to 70°F (21°C), about 30 minutes.

FERMENT Using a funnel and a strainer, pour the liquid into a sanitized fermenter. Add water as needed to fill the jug to the 1-gallon mark. Add the yeast, sanitize your hands, cover the mouth of the jug with one hand, and shake to distribute evenly. Attach a sanitized stopper and tubing to the fermenter and insert the other end of the tubing into a small bowl of sanitizing solution. The solution will begin to bubble as the yeast activates, pushing gas through the tube. Wait 2 to 3 days, until the bubbling has slowed, then replace the tubing system with an airlock. Wait 11 more days, then bottle, using the honey (see page 13 for bottling instructions).

//

SUGGESTED FOOD PAIRINGS Raw Oysters with Oyster Singel Mignonette (page 94), oyster po' boys, hamachi crudo

FOR 5 GALLONS

60-MINUTE MASH AT 152°F (67°C)
2½ gallons (9.46 liters) water, plus 6 gallons (22.71 liters) for sparging; 7.5 pounds (3401.94 grams) Belgian Pilsner malt; 1 pound (453.59 grams) Cara-Pils malt

60-MINUTE BOIL 0.5 ounce (14.17 grams) Sorachi Ace hops; 15 fresh oysters in the shell, rinsed; 1 ounce (28.35 grams) Saaz hops; 0.5 ounce (14.17 grams) Spaltz hops

FERMENT Belgian ale yeast, such as Safbrew T-58; 1 cup (340 grams) honey, for bottling

RAW OYSTERS WITH OYSTER SINGEL MIGNONETTE

MAKES 4 OUNCES SAUCE

2 oz (0.06 l) red wine vinegar

2 oz (0.06 l) Oyster Singel (page 92) or other light, flavorful beer

½ shallot, minced

Fresh cracked pepper

2 dozen shucked oysters on the half-shell

WHILE STROLLING THROUGH OUR LOCAL FARMER'S MARKETS, WE'VE ALWAYS EYED THE OYSTERS BUT ROUTINELY SHIED AWAY. THEY JUST SEEMED LIKE SOMETHING TO LEAVE TO THE PROS. BUT OVER TIME WE REALIZED THAT WHEN DEALING WITH RAW SEAFOOD, A TRUSTWORTHY FISHMONGER IS ALL YOU NEED. SO ONE AFTERNOON WE PICKED UP AN OYSTER KNIFE (AND A CUT-PROOF GLOVE) AND STARTED SHUCKING. BEER QUICKLY FOUND ITS WAY ONTO OUR OYSTERS, AND THERE WAS NO BETTER CHOICE THAN OUR OYSTER SINGEL TO BLEND WITH THE DEEP, DARK TANG OF RED WINE VINEGAR AND SHALLOTS. DRIZZLE ATOP PRISTINELY FRESH OYSTERS FOR A CLASSIC AFTERNOON IN THE KITCHEN.

//

1 Whisk all ingredients (except the oysters) in a small bowl. Drizzle over shucked oysters.

FARMHOUSE ALE RISOTTO

SERVES 4

1 cup (0.24 l) Farmhouse Ale (page 68) or other light-bodied ale

2 cups (0.47 l) chicken or vegetable stock

1 Tbsp (7 g) unsalted butter

1 garlic clove, finely chopped

½ small onion, finely chopped

1 cup (220 g) Arborio rice

¼ cup (28.35 g) shredded Parmesan

Salt and pepper

WE'RE OFTEN SHOCKED WHEN WE DISCOVER A NEW WAY TO INTRODUCE BEER INTO A DISH WE LOVE, ESPECIALLY WHEN IT'S A NO-BRAINER AFTER TASTING THE FINISHED PRODUCT. TASTING RISOTTO COOKED WITH OUR FARMHOUSE ALE IS ONE OF THOSE HEAD-SMACKINGLY OBVIOUS MOMENTS. WE MAY NEVER MAKE RISOTTO SANS BEER AGAIN.

1   In a medium pot bring the ale and stock to a simmer.

2   In a separate heavy-bottomed pot, melt the butter over medium heat, add the garlic and onion, and cook until the onion is translucent. Add the rice and cook for 1 minute, stirring constantly. Reduce the heat to medium-low.

3   Add the simmering stock/beer mixture 1 cup at a time, stirring until each cup is absorbed before adding the next. This should take about 25 minutes. You want the risotto to be super-creamy but the rice to still hold its shape.

4   When all the liquid has been absorbed into the rice, turn off the heat and stir in the Parmesan. Add salt and pepper to taste. Serve immediately.

MOULES À LA BIÈRE

SERVES 2

2 Tbsp (28 g) butter

2 shallots, diced

½ tsp (.78 g) hot red pepper flakes

¾ cup (0.18 l) Bruxelles Blonde (page 102) or other light Belgian ale

3 lb (1360.78 g) mussels, scrubbed and debearded

3 Tbsp (11.25 g) chopped fresh flat-leaf parsley

Frites, or crusty bread, for serving

NO TRIP TO BELGIUM IS COMPLETE WITHOUT TWO THINGS. THE FIRST IS AN INSANE AMOUNT OF FRENCH FRIES WITH MORE KINDS OF MAYONNAISE THAN YOU CAN COUNT. THE SECOND IS MUSSELS, AND OUR FAVORITE WAY TO COOK THEM IS IN BEER, WHICH KEEPS THEM TENDER AND RICH IN FLAVOR. ADDING RED PEPPER FLAKES GIVES THEM A SPICY KICK, AND CHOPPED PARSLEY PROVIDES AN HERBAL FRESHNESS THAT PLAYS NICELY AGAINST THE MALT SWEETNESS AND HOP BITTERNESS OF A LIGHT BELGIAN ALE.

THIS RECIPE SERVES TWO BUT CAN EASILY BE DOUBLED OR TRIPLED (AND YOUR BREW POT IS A PERFECT VESSEL TO HOLD ALL YOUR MUSSELS).

///

1 Melt the butter in a large pot over medium heat. Add the shallots and red pepper flakes and cook, stirring occasionally, until the shallots begins to soften, about 5 minutes.

2 Add the beer and mussels, turn the heat to high, and cover the pot. Cook, shaking the pot occasionally, until the mussels open, about 10 minutes. Remove from the heat.

3 Ladle the mussels into serving bowls, pour the sauce over, and scatter with parsley. Serve with frites or crusty bread.

SHANDY ICE POPS

MAKES 8 ICE POPS

½ cup (112 g) sugar
½ cup (0.12 l) water
¼ cup (0.06 l) lemon juice
1½ cups (0.35 l) light, flavorful
  beer

SHANDIES, THE LEMONADE-SPIKED, OFFICIAL BEER COCKTAIL OF SUMMER, GET EVEN MORE REFRESHING IN THIS FROZEN SPINOFF. THIS ADULTS-ONLY ICE POP COMBINES THE TART-NESS OF LEMON WITH A LIGHT, FLAVORFUL BEER (WE LOVE USING THE MULBERRY WHEAT, PAGE 41) AND JUST ENOUGH SUGAR TO MAKE IT THE PERFECT SUMMER TREAT.

1 In a small saucepan, heat the sugar and water over medium-high heat until a boil is reached, whisking until the sugar has completely dissolved, to make a simple syrup. Turn off the heat, and let cool for 2 minutes.

2 Add the lemon juice and beer and whisk until well blended.

3 Pour into ice pop molds, filling them three quarters of the way. Add Popsicle sticks and freeze for at least 4 hours.

FALL
FEELS LIKE A
back-to-school
SELECTION

• ★ • ////////////// • ★ •

The fall always feels like back-to-school time (no matter how long we've been out of it). We've packed our fall selections with mildly educational, historically inspired recipes, from a traditional Kriek to a 1945 Mild re-created from a brewer's original hand-scrawled notes.

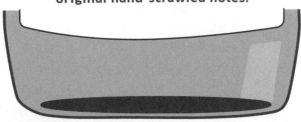

THE BREWERIES
THAT INSPIRED OUR BREWS

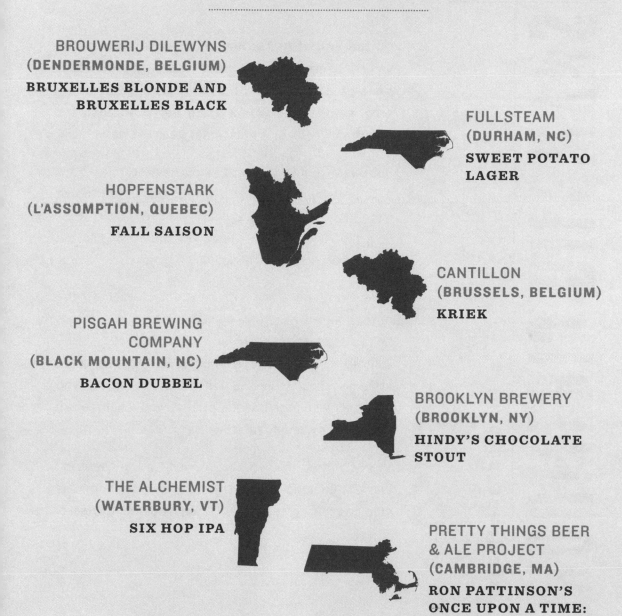

**BROUWERIJ DILEWYNS
(DENDERMONDE, BELGIUM)**

**BRUXELLES BLONDE AND
BRUXELLES BLACK**

**FULLSTEAM
(DURHAM, NC)**

**SWEET POTATO
LAGER**

**HOPFENSTARK
(L'ASSOMPTION, QUEBEC)**

FALL SAISON

**CANTILLON
(BRUSSELS, BELGIUM)**

KRIEK

**PISGAH BREWING
COMPANY
(BLACK MOUNTAIN, NC)**

BACON DUBBEL

**BROOKLYN BREWERY
(BROOKLYN, NY)**

**HINDY'S CHOCOLATE
STOUT**

**THE ALCHEMIST
(WATERBURY, VT)**

SIX HOP IPA

**PRETTY THINGS BEER
& ALE PROJECT
(CAMBRIDGE, MA)**

**RON PATTINSON'S
ONCE UPON A TIME:
1945 MILD**

PLUS: BEER & BACON MAC & CHEESE • ABBEY ONION SOUP •
BEER BEEF JERKY

BROUWERIJ DILEWYNS

DENDERMONDE, BELGIUM

BREWERY

On the wall of the Brouwerij Dilewyns, makers of Vicaris beers, is a document from 1875 in which Anne-Cathérine Dilewyns's great-great-great-great-great-grandmother Anna listed her profession for the official record: Professional Beer Brewer.

But this was not a brewery like Schlenkerla (see page 140) or Jenlain (see page 28) that was passed down from generation to generation. It never found itself pouring beers through wars or revolutions. Only the spirit of brewing was passed down over time.

Anne-Cathérine, along with her father, kicked off the new venture by serving homemade beer at festivals before starting to brew larger batches at a nearby contract brewery. She learned Italian so she could effectively communicate with the craftsmen who eventually built the brewhouse that would help return her family's name to beer.

In 2011, they opened the brewery. Anne-Cathérine was 24. Equipped with a master's in economics, she studied brewing at night and then industrial engineer-

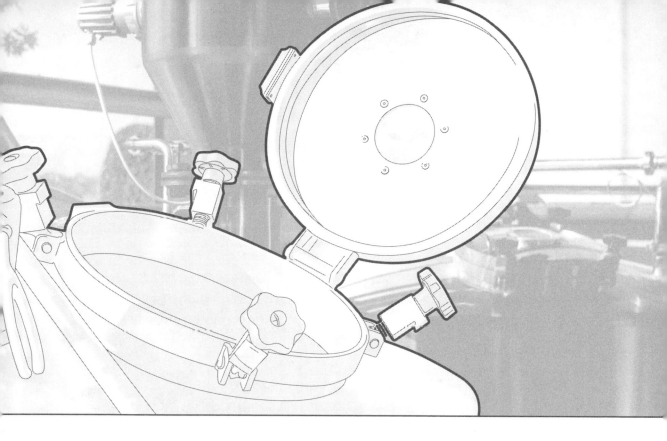

ing before she and her father, a dentist-turned-brewer, began scaling up his original recipes to become the newest brewery in a country saturated with storied, world-renowned breweries.

Five generations and one completely redefined beer landscape removed, the Dilewyns were once again making great Belgian beers.

ONE OF THE MOST INVENTIVE BEERS BREWED BY DILEWYNS IS A TRIPEL GUEUZE, WHICH COMBINES A HIGH-ALCOHOL BELGIAN TRIPEL WITH A FUNKY, BLENDED LAMBIC.

BRUXELLES BLONDE

6% ABV

60-MINUTE MASH AT 152°F (67°C)

2¼ qt (2.27 l) water, plus 1 gal (3.79 l) for sparging

1.5 lb (680.39 g) Belgian Pilsner malt

0.3 lb (136.08 g) Belgian Biscuit malt

0.2 lb (90.72 g) Caramel 15 malt

0.1 lb (45.36 g) Belgian Munich malt

0.1 lb (45.36 g) torrified wheat

*All grains should be milled (see page 15).

60-MINUTE BOIL

0.3 oz (8.5 g) Styrian Golding hops, divided into thirds

FERMENT

Belgian ale yeast, such as Safale S-33 (see note, page 16)

3 Tbsp (63 g) honey, for bottling

BELGIAN BLONDES ARE ARGUABLY THE PERFECT BEERS. IF WE WERE SOMEHOW COMMISSIONED TO STOCK ALL PICNIC BASKETS AND BASEBALL STADIUMS WITH BEER, YOU'D BE SURE TO FIND PLENTY OF BLONDES IN BOTTLES. THAT'S BECAUSE THEY'RE EVERYTHING WE LOOK FOR IN AN EASY-DRINKING YET FLAVORFUL BEER. BREWED WITH ONLY THE ESSENTIALS, THEY PROVIDE A SUBTLE GLIMPSE INTO WHAT MAKES UP THE FLAVORS THAT POUR FROM YOUR PREFERRED TULIP GLASS. BARELY SWEET FROM A BLEND OF WHEAT AND MALTED BARLEY WITH AN EARTHY, AT TIMES SPICY, HOP AROMA, OURS IS A FRESH TASTE OF THE SEASON.

MASH In a medium stockpot, heat 2¼ quarts (2.27 liters) water over high heat to 160°F (70°C). Add all the malts and stir gently. The temperature should reduce to 150°F (66°C) within 1 minute. Turn off the heat. Steep the grains for 60 minutes between 144°F and 152°F (62°C and 67°C). Every 10 minutes, stir and take the temperature. If the grains get too cold, turn the heat to high and stir until the temperature rises to that range, then turn off the heat. With 10 minutes left, in a second medium stockpot heat 1 gallon (3.79 liters) water to 170°F (77°C). After the grains have steeped for 60 minutes, turn the heat to high and stir until the temperature reaches 170°F (77°C). Turn off the heat.

SPARGE Place a fine-mesh strainer over a stockpot and pour the grains into the strainer, reserving the liquid. Pour the 1 gallon (3.79 liters) of 170°F (77°C) water over the grains. Recirculate the collected liquid through the grains once.

BOIL Return the pot with the liquid to the stove and bring to a boil over high heat. When the liquid starts to foam, reduce the heat to a slow rolling boil and add one third of the Styrian Golding hops. Add another third of the hops after 30 minutes and the final third after 45 minutes. Prepare an ice bath by stopping the sink and filling it halfway with water and ice. At the 60-minute mark, turn off the heat. Place the pot in the ice bath and cool to 70°F (21°C), about 30 minutes.

FERMENT Using a funnel and a strainer, pour the liquid into a sanitized fermenter. Add water as needed to fill the jug to the 1-gallon mark. Add the yeast, sanitize your hands, cover the mouth of the jug with one hand, and shake to distribute evenly. Attach a sanitized stopper and tubing to the fermenter and insert the other end of the tubing into a small bowl of sanitizing solution. The solution will begin to bubble as the yeast activates, pushing gas through the tube. Wait 2 to 3 days, until the bubbling has slowed, then replace the tubing system with an airlock. Wait 11 more days, then bottle, using the honey (see page 13 for bottling instructions).

//

SUGGESTED FOOD PAIRINGS Moules à la Bière (page 96), frites with mayo, washed-rind sheep's-milk cheese

FOR 5 GALLONS
60-MINUTE MASH AT 152°F (67°C)
2.8 gallons (10.65 liters) water, plus 1 gallon (3.79 liters) for sparging; 7.5 pounds (3401.94 grams) Belgian Pilsner malt; 1.5 pounds (680.38 grams) Belgian Biscuit malt; 1 pound (453.59 grams) Caramel 15 malt; 0.5 pound (226.8 grams) Belgian Munich malt; 0.5 pound (226.8 grams) torrified wheat

60-MINUTE BOIL 1.5 ounces (42.52 grams) Styrian Golding hops, divided into thirds

FERMENT Belgian ale yeast, such as Safale S-33; 1 cup (340 grams) honey, for bottling

VARIATIONS

HIBISCUS BLONDE
For a delightfully floral nose and bright fruit flavor, add ¼ cup (10 grams) dried hibiscus flowers 57 minutes into the boil; 1 cup (50 grams) for the 5-gallon variation.

CANDIED GINGER BLONDE
For a light ginger nose and dry ginger-ale-like body, add 2 pieces (14 grams) candied ginger 30 minutes into the boil; 10 pieces (70 grams) for the 5-gallon variation.

STRAWBERRY BLONDE
For a fruit-forward strawberry aroma and lightly tart body, add 1 cup (152 grams) chopped strawberries into the fermenter; 5 cups (760 grams) for the 5-gallon variation.

CILANTRO AND LIME BLONDE
For an herbaceous complement to Mexican fare, add ½ cup (20 grams) chopped fresh cilantro and 1 dried lime peel 55 minutes into the boil; 2½ cups (100 grams) cilantro and 3 dried lime peels for the 5-gallon variation.

BRUXELLES BLACK

6% ABV

60-MINUTE MASH AT 152°F (67°C)

2½ qt (2.37 l) water, plus 1 gal (3.79 l) for sparging

1.6 lb (725.75 g) Belgian Pilsner malt

0.2 lb (90.72 g) Belgian Munich malt

0.2 lb (90.72 g) Belgian Biscuit malt

0.2 lb (90.72 g) Black malt

*All grains should be milled (see page 15).

60-MINUTE BOIL

0.15 oz (4.25 g) Pacific Jade hops, divided into thirds

0.1 oz (2.83 g) Saaz hops

⅓ cup (112 g) honey

FERMENT

Belgian ale yeast, such as Safale S-33 (see note, page 16)

3 Tbsp (63 g) honey, for bottling

IT CAN SOMETIMES APPEAR THAT BELGIAN BEERS HAVE BEGUN TAKING ON A CLASSIC, STATELY QUALITY, BUT IT'S DIFFICULT TO ARGUE WITH A BREWING TRADITION WHERE CORNER BODEGAS CAN BOAST BEER STOCKS THAT MAKE BOTTLE SHOPS ACROSS THE GLOBE BLUSH. WITH BRUXELLES BLACK, THAT TRADITION INSPIRED US TO THINK UP A NEW CLASSIC. THIS DARK BELGIAN-STYLE ALE IS BREWED WITH BELGIAN MALTS, HONEY, AS WELL AS SAAZ AND PACIFIC JADE HOPS. SAAZ IS DELIGHTFULLY SPICY AND EASY ON THE NOSE, BUT THE ADDITION OF THE AGGRESSIVELY BLACK PEPPER–SCENTED NEW ZEALAND–GROWN PACIFIC JADE HOPS CONTRIBUTES THE ADDITIONAL BITTERNESS AND AROMA NEEDED TO BALANCE THIS BEER'S RICHER MALT BASE.

MASH In a medium stockpot, heat 2½ quarts (2.37 liters) water over high heat to 160°F (70°C). Add all the malts and stir gently. The temperature should reduce to 150°F (66°C) within 1 minute. Turn off the heat. Steep the grains for 60 minutes between 144°F and 152°F (62°C and 67°C). Every 10 minutes, stir and take the temperature. If the grains get too cold, turn the heat to high and stir until the temperature rises to that range, then turn off the heat. With 10 minutes left, in a second medium stockpot heat 1 gallon (3.79 liters) water to 170°F (77°C). After the grains have steeped for 60 minutes, turn the heat to high and stir until the temperature reaches 170°F (77°C). Turn off the heat.

SPARGE Place a fine-mesh strainer over a stock-pot and pour the grains into the strainer, reserving the liquid. Pour the 1 gallon (3.79 liters) of 170°F (77°C) water over the grains. Recirculate the collected liquid through the grains once.

BOIL Return the pot with the liquid to the stove and bring to a boil over high heat. When the liquid starts to foam, reduce the heat to a slow rolling boil and add one third of the Pacific Jade hops. Add another third of the Pacific Jade hops after 30 minutes and the remainder after 50 minutes. Prepare an ice bath by stopping the sink and filling it halfway with water and ice. Add the Saaz hops after 59 minutes. At the 60-minute mark, turn off the heat, add the ⅓ cup (112 grams) honey, and stir to dissolve. Place the pot in the ice bath and cool to 70°F (21°C), about 30 minutes.

FERMENT Using a funnel and a strainer, pour the liquid into a sanitized fermenter. Add water as needed to fill the jug to the 1-gallon mark. Add the yeast, sanitize your hands, cover the mouth of the jug with one hand, and shake to distribute evenly. Attach a sanitized stopper and tubing to the fermenter and insert the other end of the tubing into a small bowl of sanitizing solution. The solution will begin to bubble as the yeast activates, pushing gas through the tube. Wait 2 to 3 days, until the bubbling has slowed, then replace the tubing system with an airlock. Wait 11 more days, then bottle, using the honey (see page 13 for bottling instructions).

SUGGESTED FOOD PAIRINGS Abbey Onion Soup (page 136), carbonnade, Beer Beef Jerky (page 137)

FOR 5 GALLONS

60-MINUTE MASH AT 152°F (67°C)
3¼ gallons (12.3 liters) water, plus 4 gallons (15.14 liters) for sparging; 8 pounds (3628.74 grams) Belgian Pilsner malt; 1 pound (453.59 grams) Belgian Munich malt; 1 pound (453.59 grams) Belgian Biscuit malt; 1 pound (453.59 grams) Black malt

60-MINUTE BOIL 0.75 ounce (21.26 grams) Pacific Jade hops, divided into thirds; 0.5 ounce (14.17 grams) Saaz hops; 1⅔ cups (566 grams) honey

FERMENT Belgian ale yeast, such as Safale S-33; 1 cup (340 grams) honey, for bottling

HOPFENSTARK

L'ASSOMPTION, QUEBEC

BREWERY

If you think of beer styles as musical styles, you may start to understand the approach to brewing taken by Frederick Cormier, the founder and brewmaster of Hopfenstark. "I try to perfect one style at a time," says Fred in the Montreal tasting room outpost of his Quebecois brewery.

It's uncommon for one brewery to make excellent representations of beer from across the world that, on one tap list, can fully capture the rich malt depth of German brews, the lively spice of Belgian ones, and the warmth of beers that come out of Britain's brewing tradition.

But simply re-creating styles from across the globe would not be reason enough to track down a Hopfenstark bottle. It's what happens after a style is mastered that truly stands out. Styles collide, blend, and influence one another. Hopfenstark's Boson de Higgs, for example, fits nowhere neatly. It's best described as a Berliner-rauch-saison combining the tartness of a Berliner weisse, the smoked malt of a rauchbier, and the spicy yeast character of a saison into one incredibly complex glass of beer.

Just like learning to play an instrument, perfecting the minutiae instilled in each style of beer requires discipline. Drinking is not allowed until brew day is complete, and brewers spend months practicing the best way to turn a lever. Brewing techniques as well as the regional ingredients must be mastered.

But it's all worth it when tasting the finished product as the tiniest notes come together to create the perfect two-and-a-half-minute song. Fred is the bandleader, and the bar is his stage.

WHILE THE BEER IS BREWED WELL OUTSIDE CITY LIMITS, YOU'LL OFTEN FIND FRED MANNING THE PLAYLIST AT STATION HO.ST—HOPFENSTARK'S BAR NEAR PARC LA FONTAINE IN MONTREAL.

FALL SAISON

5% ABV

60-MINUTE MASH AT 152°F (67°C)

2 qt (1.89 l) water, plus 1 gal (3.79 l) for sparging

1.5 lb (680.39 g) Belgian Pilsner malt

0.3 lb (136.08 g) Vienna malt

0.2 lb (90.72 g) Caramunich malt

*All grains should be milled (see page 15).

60-MINUTE BOIL

0.2 oz (5.67 g) Styrian Golding hops, divided in half

0.2 oz (5.67 g) Saaz hops

FERMENT

Belgian ale yeast, such as Wyeast Belgian Saison or Safale T-58 (see note, page 16)

3 Tbsp (63 g) honey, for bottling

WHEN FALL COMES AROUND, WE END UP DRINKING A LOT OF MALTIER BEERS. PUMPKIN BEERS, HARVEST ALES—CALL THEM WHAT YOU WANT. WE LOVE THEM, BUT THEY CAN LEAVE OUR PALATES THIRSTING FOR SOMETHING LIGHTER. SAISONS ARE TRADITIONALLY MEANT FOR SUMMER DRINKING, BUT FOR OUR FALL SAISON WE THOUGHT THAT SPLITTING THE DIFFERENCE BETWEEN THE MIGHTY MALT BACKBONE OF AUTUMN AND THE CRISP AND DRY CHARACTER OF A TRADITIONAL SAISON WOULD BE THE IDEAL RESET BUTTON FOR A FALL EVENING ON THE ROOFTOP. THE ADDITION OF CARAMUNICH AND VIENNA MALTS GIVES THIS BEER A GENTLE MALTINESS AND WARM COLOR IDEAL FOR THOSE EARLY NIGHTS OF SWEATER SEASON.

MASH In a medium stockpot, heat 2 quarts (1.89 liters) water over high heat to 160°F (70°C). Add all the malts and stir gently. The temperature should reduce to 150°F (66°C) within 1 minute. Turn off the heat. Steep the grains for 60 minutes between 144°F and 152°F (62°C and 67°C). Every 10 minutes, stir and take the temperature. If the grains get too cold, turn the heat to high and stir until the temperature rises to that range, then turn off the heat. With 10 minutes left, in a second medium stockpot heat 1 gallon (3.79 liters) water to 170°F (77°C). After the grains have steeped for 60 minutes, turn the heat to high and stir until the temperature reaches 170°F (77°C). Turn off the heat.

SPARGE Place a fine-mesh strainer over a stock-pot and pour the grains into the strainer, reserving the liquid. Pour the 1 gallon (3.79 liters) of 170°F (77°C) water over the grains. Recirculate the collected liquid through the grains once.

BOIL Return the pot with the liquid to the stove and bring to a boil over high heat. When the liquid starts to foam, reduce the heat to a slow rolling boil and add half of the Styrian Golding hops. Add the remaining Styrian Golding hops after 30 minutes. Add the Saaz hops after 55 minutes. Prepare an ice bath by stopping the sink and filling it halfway with water and ice. At the 60-minute mark, turn off the heat. Place the pot in the ice bath and cool to 70°F (21°C), about 30 minutes.

FERMENT Using a funnel and a strainer, pour the liquid into a sanitized fermenter. Add water as needed to fill the jug to the 1-gallon mark. Add the yeast, sanitize your hands, cover the mouth of the jug with one hand, and shake to distribute evenly. Attach a sanitized stopper and tubing to the fermenter and insert the other end of the tubing into a small bowl of sanitizing solution. The solution will begin to bubble as the yeast activates, pushing gas through the tube. Wait 2 to 3 days, until the bubbling has slowed, then replace the tubing system with an airlock. Wait 11 more days, then bottle, using the honey (see page 13 for bottling instructions).

//

SUGGESTED FOOD PAIRINGS Venison sausage, roasted cauliflower, mushroom soup

FOR 5 GALLONS

60-MINUTE MASH AT 152°F (67°C.)
2½ gallons (9.46 liters) water, plus 5 gallons (18.93 liters) for sparging; 7.5 pounds (3401.94 grams) Belgian Pilsner malt; 1.5 pounds (680.39 grams) Vienna malt; 1 pound (453.59 grams) Caramunich malt

60-MINUTE BOIL 1 ounce (28.35 grams) Styrian Golding hops, divided in half; 1 ounce (28.35 grams) Saaz hops

FERMENT Belgian ale yeast, such as Wyeast Belgian Saison or Safale T-58; 1 cup (340 grams) honey, for bottling

PISGAH BREWING CO.

BLACK MOUNTAIN, NC

BREWERY

People love beer. And they love bacon. So we should not have been surprised by the sheer frequency of a question we've been asked from day one: "How would I add bacon to a beer?" To which our standing reply has always been, "Don't."

We typically recommend using smoked barley (see Schlenkerla, page 140, and Ranger Creek, page 62) to produce the smoke and caramel malt that mimics the hearty body and sweet taste of perfectly crisp bacon. And for the people who would say, "No, really. I'm putting bacon in my beer whether you like it or not," we might have gone as far as recommending the addition of salt or charred wood to a beer. Basically anything and everything except adding actual piggy parts.

But when we tasted Pisgah Brewing Company's Benton's Bacon Snout, we were forced to revise our thought process to "Why not?" and "How?"

And really, why not? We've added lobster shells to beer as well as whole oysters (see Oyster Singel, page 92). We've worked around the fat content (which can spoil beer and kill foam) in our Peanut Butter Porter. We routinely seek out and think up beers with weird and challenging ingredients, but it wasn't until tasting this dark, rich, and, for lack of a better term, liquid bacon that we were ready to go full snout and whole hog.

Throughout culinary history, a lot of good, tasty things start with someone asking "Why not?" Which is pretty much how Jeremy Austin and the Pisgah brewers arrived at their Bacon Snout. They start off with some of the finest bacon in the States (Benton's Smoky Mountain Country Ham out of Tennessee, which counts Momofuku's David Chang and David Kahan of The Publican in Chicago as devotees), trim it down, and add it to a second cold fermentation. The beer mingles with the bacon before being pumped out into kegs and pumped up with CO_2.

> "I'M PUTTING BACON IN MY BEER WHETHER YOU LIKE IT OR NOT."
>
> —TOO MANY CUSTOMERS TO COUNT

BACON DUBBEL

6.2% ABV

60-MINUTE MASH AT 152°F (67°C)

2¼ qt (2.13 l) water, plus 1 gal (3.79 l) for sparging

1.5 lb (680.39 g) Belgian Pilsner malt

0.25 lb (113.4 g) Munich malt

0.15 lb (68.04 g) Special B malt

0.15 lb (68.04 g) Caramel 40 malt

0.05 lb (22.68 g) Caramel 120 malt

*All grains should be milled (see page 15).

60-MINUTE BOIL

0.4 oz (11.34 g) Hallertau hops, divided into quarters

0.2 lb (90.72 g) Belgian Candi Sugar

FERMENT

Belgian ale yeast, such as Safale S-33 (see note, page 16)

3 strips (90.72 g) high-quality bacon, well trimmed and cooked (see prep)

3 Tbsp (63 g) maple syrup, for bottling

A DUBBEL IS A DARKER BELGIAN-STYLE ALE, A LITTLE MORE ALCOHOLIC THAN A SINGEL AND A LITTLE LESS THAN A TRIPEL. TRUTH IN ADVERTISING FOR MONKS. DUBBELS COMPLEMENT HEARTIER FLAVORS REALLY WELL AND FEATURE A BIT OF SWEETNESS THAT PAIRS PERFECTLY WITH BACON. FOR OUR STOVETOP VERSION WE RECOMMEND USING THE HIGHEST-QUALITY BACON YOU CAN FIND, TRIMMING IT AGGRESSIVELY, AND DRYING IT OUT TO REMOVE AS MUCH FAT AS YOU CAN. THE RESULT IS A PROPERLY SMOKY, HEARTY, DELICIOUS 100 PERCENT PURE BACON BEER.

PREP Preheat the oven to 375°F (190°C). Trim the fat from the bacon. Arrange the bacon in a single layer on a wire rack set on top of a baking sheet. Bake for 15 to 20 minutes, until the bacon is dry but not burnt. Remove from the oven and, using a paper towel, pat the bacon to absorb any oil. Set aside.

MASH In a medium stockpot, heat 2¼ quarts (2.13 liters) water over high heat to 160°F (70°C). Add all the malts and stir gently. The temperature should reduce to 150°F (66°C) within 1 minute. Turn off the heat. Steep the grains for 60 minutes between 144°F and 152°F (62°C and 67°C). Every 10 minutes, stir and take the temperature. If the grains get too cold, turn the heat to high and stir until the temperature rises to that range, then turn off the heat. With 10 minutes left, in a second medium stockpot heat 1 gallon (3.79 liters) water to 170°F (77°C). After the grains have steeped for 60 minutes, turn the heat to high and stir until the temperature reaches 170°F (77°C). Turn off the heat.

SPARGE Place a fine-mesh strainer over a stock-pot and pour the grains into the strainer, reserving the liquid. Pour the 1 gallon (3.79 liters) of 170°F (77°C) water over the grains. Recirculate the collected liquid through the grains once.

BOIL Return the pot with the liquid to the stove and bring to a boil over high heat. When the liquid starts to foam, reduce the heat to a slow rolling boil and add one half of the Hallertau hops. Add one quarter of the Hallertau hops after 30 minutes. Add the remaining quarter Hallertau hops and Belgian Candi Sugar after 55 minutes, stirring to dissolve the sugar. Prepare an ice bath by stopping the sink and filling it halfway with water and ice. At the 60-minute mark, turn off the heat. Place the pot in the ice bath and cool to 70°F (21°C), about 30 minutes.

FERMENT Using a funnel and a strainer, pour the liquid into a sanitized fermenter. Add water as needed to fill the jug to the 1-gallon mark. Add the yeast, sanitize your hands, cover the mouth of the jug with one hand, and shake to distribute evenly. Attach a sanitized stopper and tubing to the fermenter and insert the other end of the tubing into a small bowl of sanitizing solution. The solution will begin to bubble as the yeast activates, pushing gas through the tube. Wait 2 to 3 days, until the bubbling has slowed, add the bacon directly to the fermenter, then replace the tubing system with an airlock. Wait 11 more days, then bottle, using the maple syrup (see page 13 for bottling instructions).

//

SUGGESTED FOOD PAIRINGS BLT sandwiches, Beer & Bacon Mac & Cheese (page 135), salted chocolate

FOR 5 GALLONS

60-MINUTE MASH AT 152°F (67°C)

2¾ gallons (10.41 liters) water, plus 5 gallons (18.93 liters) for sparging; 7.5 pounds (3401.94 grams) Belgian Pilsner malt; 1.25 pounds (566.99 grams) Munich malt; 0.75 pound (340.19 grams) Special B malt; 0.75 pound (340.19 grams) Caramel 40 malt; 0.25 pound (113.4 grams) Caramel 120 malt

60-MINUTE BOIL

2 ounces (56.7 grams) Hallertau hops, divided into quarters; 1 pound (453.59 grams) Belgian Candi Sugar

FERMENT

Belgian ale yeast, such as Safale S-33; 1 pound (453.59 grams) bacon, well trimmed and cooked (see prep); 1 cup (340 grams) maple syrup, for bottling

THE ALCHEMIST

WATERBURY, VT

BREWERY

When Tropical Storm Irene destroyed John and Jen Kimmish's seven-barrel brewpub overnight, they had to change gears, quickly. What they lost was the place where they had brewed and experimented for eight years, creating dozens of beers of all styles.

What remained was their brand-new expansion project, a cannery up the road (and around the corner from the original Ben & Jerry's factory) that was set to open just days after the storm. It went untouched by the floods that took much of the area by surprise.

Brewing three shifts per day, four days per week, the cannery churns out only one beer, Heady Topper, a double IPA that many regard as the perfect expression of hops. Each sip fills your senses with plumes of citrus, resinous pine, and wildflowers.

When you spend so much time creating one beer, it must be perfect. Like bees making honey, the brewery buzzes with the constant shuffling of beer from one shiny, tightly packed stainless-steel tank to another. Beer never sleeps. In a brewhouse, beer is constantly changing throughout for the month it takes to become real.

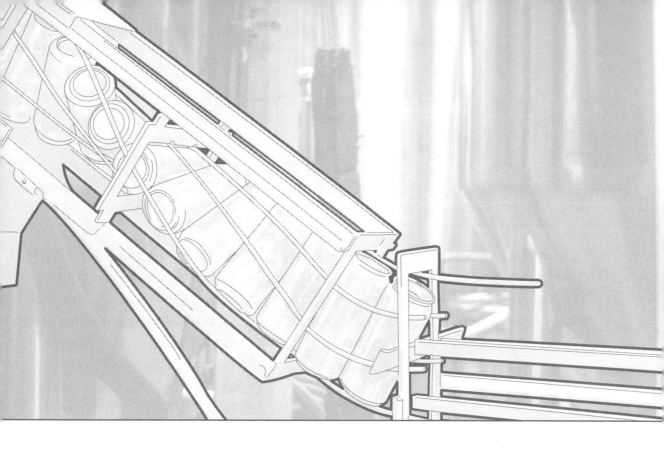

Fortunately for bees, honey keeps until winter. The Alchemist pumps out cans of Heady Topper all week—until they can't. Sellouts are the norm. There is no saving beer for winter when it's this fresh and all of northern Vermont is lined up out your door.

And while the long lines, inevitable sellouts, and illicit black market crossing state boundaries sometimes make it difficult to remember we're all simply talking about beer, it's making the best beer possible that the staff at The Alchemist lives for.

TO SAMPLE SOME OF VERMONT'S BEST BEERS AND SEE WHERE THE ALCHEMIST GOT ITS START, HEAD TO PROHIBITION PIG IN WATERBURY.

SIX HOP IPA

6% ABV

60-MINUTE MASH AT 152°F (67°C)

2½ qt (2.37 l) water, plus 1 gal (3.79 l) for sparging

1.75 lb (793.79 g) American 2-row malt

0.4 lb (181.44 g) Vienna malt

0.15 lb (68.04 g) Caramel 20 malt

*All grains should be milled (see page 15).

75-MINUTE BOIL

0.1 oz (2.83 g) Amarillo hops

0.1 oz (2.83 g) Chinook hops

0.1 oz (2.83 g) Simcoe hops

0.1 oz (2.83 g) Citra hops

0.1 oz (2.83 g) Warrior hops

0.1 oz (2.83 g) Galaxy hops

FERMENT

America ale yeast, such as Safale S-05 (see note, page 16)

3 Tbsp (63 g) honey, for bottling

THE ONLY THING THAT HEADY TOPPER AND THIS IPA HAVE IN COMMON IS THE NUMBER OF HOPS IN EACH. FOR US, BEER IS AS MUCH ABOUT THE PLACE AS THE INGREDIENTS AND TECHNIQUES USED TO PRODUCE IT. YOU CAN'T BOTTLE THE ROLLING HILLS, COVERED BRIDGES, AND PERMEATING STENCH OF ROADSIDE COW DUNG THAT MAKE NORTHERN VERMONT THE BUCOLIC OASIS TO WHICH WE CITY DWELLERS ESCAPE FOR MUCH-NEEDED MOMENTS SEPARATED FROM CELL-PHONE SERVICE. SURROUNDINGS HAVE A WAY OF FILLING OUR CUPS, ENSURING HEADY TOPPER A SPECIAL PLACE IN THE AMERICAN BEER LANDSCAPE. WE WANTED TO BREW A BEER THAT TASTES LIKE STANDING IN THE MIDDLE OF A GRASSY FIELD IN VERMONT. TO DO THAT, WE WHIPPED UP A MOSTLY AMERICAN SIX-HOP BLEND (WITH THE SOLE EXCEPTION OF THE PASSIONFRUITY GALAXY HOP FROM AUSTRALIA) TO BE ADDED AT SIX DIFFERENT TIMES, INCLUDING ONE DRY HOP ADDITION IN THE FRIDGE.

///

MASH In a medium stockpot, heat 2½ quarts (2.37 liters) water over high heat to 160°F (70°C). Add all the malts and stir gently. The temperature should reduce to 150°F (66°C) within 1 minute. Turn off the heat. Steep the grains for 60 minutes between 144°F and 152°F (62°C and 67°C). Every 10 minutes, stir and take the temperature. If the grains get too cold, turn the heat to high and stir until the temperature rises to that range, then turn off the heat. With 10 minutes left, in a second medium stockpot heat 1 gallon

(3.79 liters) water to 170°F (77°C). After the grains have steeped for 60 minutes, turn the heat to high and stir until the temperature reaches 170°F (77°C). Turn off the heat.

SPARGE Place a fine-mesh strainer over a stockpot and pour the grains into the strainer, reserving the liquid. Pour the 1 gallon (3.79 liters) of 170°F (77°C) water over the grains. Recirculate the collected liquid through the grains once.

BOIL Blend all the hops together, and divide into sixths. Return the pot with the liquid to the stove and bring to a boil over high heat. When the liquid starts to foam, reduce the heat to a slow rolling boil and add one sixth of the hop blend. Add a sixth of the hop blend after 30, 60, and 70 minutes. Prepare an ice bath by stopping the sink and filling it halfway with water and ice. At the 75-minute mark, turn off the heat and add another sixth of the hop blend (reserving the final sixth for dry-hopping during fermentation). Place the pot in the ice bath and cool to 70°F (21°C), about 30 minutes.

FERMENT Using a funnel and a strainer, pour the liquid into a sanitized fermenter. Add water as needed to fill the jug to the 1-gallon mark. Add the yeast, sanitize your hands, cover the mouth of the jug with one hand, and shake to distribute evenly. Attach a sanitized stopper and tubing to the fermenter and insert the other end of the tubing into a small bowl of sanitizing solution. The solution will begin to bubble as the yeast activates, push-ing gas through the tube. Wait 2 to 3 days, until the bubbling has slowed, then replace the tubing system with an airlock. Wait 11 more days, add the remaining one sixth of the hops blend directly to the fermenter, place in the refrigerator, and cover to keep out the light. After 5 more days remove from the refrigerator and bottle, using the honey (see page 13 for bottling instructions).

//

SUGGESTED FOOD PAIRINGS Green papaya salad, Vietnamese-style wings, chicken satay

FOR 5 GALLONS

60-MINUTE MASH AT 152°F (67°C)
3¼ gallons (12.3 liters) water, plus 4 gallons (15.14 liters) for sparging; 8.75 pounds (3968.93 grams) American 2-row malt; 2 pounds (907.19 grams) Vienna malt; 0.75 pound (340.19 grams) Caramel 20 malt

75-MINUTE BOIL 0.5 ounce (14.17 grams) Amarillo hops; 0.5 ounce (14.17 grams) Chinook hops; 0.5 ounce (14.17 grams) Simcoe hops; 0.5 ounce (14.17 grams) Citra hops; 0.5 ounce (14.17 grams) Warrior hops; 0.5 ounce (14.17 grams) Galaxy hops.

FERMENT American ale yeast, such as Safale S-05; 1 cup (340 grams) honey, for bottling

FULLSTEAM

DURHAM, NC

BREWERY

When Fullsteam's chief executive optimist Sean Lilly Wilson and head brewer Chris Davis set out to make distinctly Southern beers, they didn't have a catalog of historic recipes from proud Southern brewers.

Moonshine and wine make up most of North Carolina's boozy history, so Wilson and Davis figured that with a focus on local ingredients, they could invent a new regional way of brewing. They dreamed of using only ingredients produced within 300 miles of Durham—a dream that at first seemed laughable, but is slowly changing thanks to both a fresh eye toward what ingredients can make up a beer and the rise of local hop farms and maltsters.

From wet smoking malt over hickory (the wood traditionally used in Carolina BBQ) to a winter ale spiked with community-grown persimmons to a not-entirely-serious yet surprisingly good beer made with Cheerwine (the local cherry cola), they're inching closer to a distinctly Southern beer with each new batch.

The only thing more local is something grown in your own backyard . . . literally. So the folks at Fullsteam put a call out to the community for persimmons. In the woods, bordering farms, or randomly in someone's yard is where you'll typically find persimmons growing. Native to North Carolina, persimmon trees bear fruit that is by no means considered a supermarket staple.

The request resulted in Fullsteam's Forager Series—a series of recipes relying on the local community to supply the ingredients, creating not only a distinctively Southern beer, but a Southern beer economy bridging backyards to a 10-barrel brewhouse. They've since done the same with figs and pears.

Most rewarding for Wilson is "people who say 'I never knew what a persimmon was' . . . and if beer is the vehicle for getting them to understand some of what grows here and some of our historical ingredients, then we are doing our job."

When you open up the idea of foraging, you'll start to get people coming in with a bag of fruit and saying, "Do you guys want this?" whether you've asked for it or not—but there are worse things in life than a bag of fresh Southern fruit.

FOR OUR TAKE ON A FORAGING BEER, CHECK OUT MULBERRY WHEAT (PAGE 41).

SWEET POTATO LAGER

5.5% ABV

PREP

0.8 lb (362.87 g) sweet potato

60-MINUTE MASH AT 152°F (67°C)

3 qt (2.84 l) water, plus 1 gal (3.79 l) for sparging

1.6 lb (725.75 g) English Pale malt

0.4 lb (181.44 g) pureed sweet potato (see prep)

0.2 lb (90.72 g) Caramel 10 malt

0.2 lb (90.72 g) Caramel 40 malt

*All grains should be milled (see page 15).

60-MINUTE BOIL

0.6 oz (17 g) Northern Brewer hops, divided into sixths

FERMENT

Lager yeast, such as Saflager S-23 (see note, page 16)

3 Tbsp (63 g) honey, for bottling

FEW THINGS ARE MORE DISTINCTIVELY SOUTHERN, OR FOR THAT MATTER NORTH CAROLINIAN, THAN SWEET POTATOES (THE STATE IS THE NATION'S TOP PRODUCER). TWO HUNDRED AND FIFTY POUNDS OF LOCALLY GROWN PUREED SWEET POTATOES GET THROWN INTO EVERY BATCH OF FULLSTEAM'S CARVER SWEET POTATO LAGER, MAKING UP A THIRD OF THEIR BEER'S FERMENTABLE SUGARS AS WELL AS A VERY STICKY MASH.

//

PREP Peel and chop 0.8 pound (362.87 grams) sweet potato, reserving 0.4 pound (181.44 grams). In a medium stockpot, boil 0.4 pound (181.44 grams) sweet potato in water for 20 minutes. Strain, then puree using a food processor or blender.

MASH In a medium stockpot, heat 3 quarts (2.84 liters) water over high heat to 160°F (70°C). Add all the malts and the sweet potato puree and stir gently. The temperature should reduce to 150°F (66°C) within 1 minute. Turn off the heat. Steep the grains for 60 minutes between 144°F and 152°F (62°C and 67°C). Every 10 minutes, stir and take the temperature. If the grains get too cold, turn the heat to high and stir until the temperature rises to that range, then turn off the heat. With 10 minutes left, in a second medium stockpot heat 1 gallon (3.79 liters) water to 170°F (77°C). After the grains have steeped for 60 minutes, turn the heat to high and stir until the temperature reaches 170°F (77°C). Turn off the heat.

SPARGE Place a fine-mesh strainer over a stock-pot and pour the grains into the strainer, reserving the liquid. Pour the 1 gallon (3.79 liters) of 170°F (77°C) water over the grains. Recirculate the collected liquid through the grains once.

BOIL Return the pot with the liquid to the stove and bring to a boil over high heat. When the liquid starts to foam, reduce the heat to a slow rolling boil and add one sixth of the Northern Brewer hops and the reserved 0.4 pound (181.44 grams) chopped sweet potato. Add another sixth of the Northern Brewer hops after 15 minutes, 30 minutes, 45 minutes, and 55 minutes into the boil. Prepare an ice bath by stopping the sink and filling it halfway with water and ice. At the 60-minute mark, turn off the heat and add the remaining sixth Northern Brewer hops. Place the pot in the ice bath and cool to 70°F (21°C), about 30 minutes.

FERMENT Using a funnel and a strainer, pour the liquid into a sanitized fermenter. Add water as needed to fill the jug to the 1-gallon mark. Add the yeast, sanitize your hands, cover the mouth of the jug with one hand, and shake to distribute evenly. Attach a sanitized stopper and tubing to the fermenter and insert the other end of the tubing into a small bowl of sanitizing solution. The solution will begin to bubble as the yeast activates, pushing gas through the tube. Wait 2 to 3 days, until the bubbling has slowed, then replace the tubing system with an airlock. Wait 11 more days, then bottle, using the honey (see page 13 for bottling instructions).

SUGGESTED FOOD PAIRINGS Buttermilk fried chicken, shepherd's pie, mashed sweet potatoes

FOR 5 GALLONS

PREP 4 pounds (1814.37 grams) sweet potato, peeled and chopped

60-MINUTE MASH AT 152°F (67°C) 3¾ gallons (14.2 liters) water, plus 4 gallons (15.14 liters) for sparging; 8 pounds (3628.74 grams) English Pale malt; 1 pound (453.59 grams) Caramel 10 malt; 1 pound (453.59 grams) Caramel 40 malt

60-MINUTE BOIL 3 ounces (85.05 grams) Northern Brewer hops, divided into sixths

FERMENT Lager yeast, such as Saflager S-23; 1 cup (340 grams) honey, for bottling

NOTE: While this beer calls for lager yeast, it is fermented at ale temperatures. This style is known as a California Common.

CANTILLON

BRUSSELS, BELGIUM

BREWERY

When we think of brewing with local ingredients, what usually comes to mind is barley, hops, and sometimes fruit. But what about the local ingredients you can't see? The magic that a specific place can bring to brewing creates a totally unique beer that can define a style.

When speaking of magic in beer, we mean yeast—the creepiest, coolest, most mystifying ingredient of any batch. It's in the air. It's all around us. It's wild, and it's the reason why we emphasize cleanliness while brewing. In the wrong hands, magic can be unpredictable and not-so-tasty, but when everything goes right, nothing compares.

Cantillon makes lambic beers (spontaneously fermented sour ales) and has done so in the heart of Brussels since 1900. Its beers are sour, very sour, which can surprise a few people at the end of the self-guided tours when you get to the samples. For the tour you receive a French language pamphlet and follow the brewery's pipes to figure out what's going on. While walking the brewery, you quickly realize how similar making your own beer is to traditional brewing . . . until you get to the fermenter, which, in Cantillon's case, is open to the night's air.

After the boil, beer flows into a large copper tank with no cover. The brewers then open the shutters and let the Brussels air flow over the beer. Different indigenous strains of yeast compete and ferment the beer in the process. The resulting beer has a complex blend of flavors from the competing yeasts, and the only official winner is us.

PLAN AHEAD TO ATTEND CANTILLON'S PUBLIC BREW DAY HELD ANNUALLY. THEN PLAN ANOTHER TRIP THREE YEARS LATER TO TASTE IT.

KRIEK

5.75% ABV

60-MINUTE MASH AT 152°F (67°C)

2¼ qt (2.13 l) water, plus 1 gal (3.79 l) for sparging

1.6 lb (725.75 g) Belgian Pilsner malt

0.4 lb (181.44 g) Belgian Wheat malt

0.25 lb (113.4 g) Caramel 10 malt

*All grains should be milled (see page 15).

60-MINUTE BOIL

0.2 oz (5.67 g) Saaz hops, divided in half

FERMENT

Lambic yeast blend, such as Wyeast Brettanomyces Lambicus (see note, page 16)

1 cup (240 g) sour cherries, pitted and crushed

3 Tbsp (63 g) honey, for bottling

WHILE WE DON'T TELL YOU TO LEAVE YOUR BEER IN A COPPER VESSEL AND OPEN THE SHUTTERS (OR USE STALE HOPS EXPOSED TO THE AIR FOR THREE YEARS), THIS IS STILL A PRETTY TRADITIONAL TAKE ON THE STYLE, WITH A LENGTHY FERMENTATION AND AGING PERIOD, AND SHOULD BE ATTEMPTED ONLY AFTER EARNING QUITE A FEW NOTCHES ON YOUR BREWING BELT. FOR AN EASIER INTRODUCTION TO SOUR BEERS, TRY THE LACTIC-FERMENTED BERLINER WEISSE (PAGE 22).

BUT FOR THOSE READY (AND PATIENT) BREWERS, OUR KRIEK FINISHES QUITE DRY WITH A SHARP SOURNESS TEMPERED JUST A TOUCH BY THE CHERRIES AND LIGHT MALT BACKBONE. THE LONGER YOU LET THIS ONE AGE, THE MORE BRANDY-LIKE THE CHERRY NOTES BECOME.

MASH In a medium stockpot, heat 2¼ quarts (2.13 liters) water over high heat to 160°F (70°C). Add all the malts and stir gently. The temperature should reduce to 150°F (66°C) within 1 minute. Turn off the heat. Steep the grains for 60 minutes between 144°F and 152°F (62°C and 67°C). Every 10 minutes, stir and take the temperature. If the grains get too cold, turn the heat to high and stir until the temperature rises to that range, then turn off the heat. With 10 minutes left, in a second medium stockpot heat 1 gallon (3.79 liters) water to 170°F (77°C). After the grains have steeped for 60 minutes, turn the heat to high and stir until the temperature reaches 170°F (77°C). Turn off the heat.

SPARGE Place a fine-mesh strainer over a stockpot and pour the grains into the strainer, reserving the liquid. Pour the 1 gallon (3.79 liters) of 170°F (77°C) water over the grains. Recirculate the collected liquid through the grains once.

BOIL Return the pot with the liquid to the stove and bring to a boil over high heat. When the liquid starts to foam, reduce the heat to a slow rolling boil. Add half of the Saaz hops after 50 minutes. Prepare an ice bath by stopping the sink and filling it halfway with water and ice. At the 60-minute mark, turn off the heat and add the remaining hops. Place the pot in the ice bath and cool to 70°F (21°C), about 30 minutes.

FERMENT Using a funnel and a strainer, pour the liquid into a sanitized fermenter. Add water as needed to fill the jug to the 1-gallon mark. Add the yeast, sanitize your hands, cover the mouth of the jug with one hand, and shake to distribute evenly. Attach a sanitized stopper and tubing to the fermenter and insert the other end of the tubing into a small bowl of sanitizing solution. The solution will begin to bubble as the yeast activates, pushing gas through the tube. Wait 2 to 3 days, until the bubbling has slowed, then replace the tubing system with an airlock. Wait 5 more days, then add the cherries to a second fermentation jug, siphon the beer into the fermenter on top of the cherries, and attach a sanitized stopper and airlock. Let ferment for 1 month. Siphon the beer (leaving behind the cherries) into a third fermentation jug. Let ferment for 3 more months. When the surface area is free of any bubbles, bottle, using the honey (see page 13 for bottling instructions) in Belgian-style bottles (see page 15). Age an additional 6 to 12 months in bottles.

//

SUGGESTED FOOD PAIRINGS Cheesecake, foie gras, bacon-wrapped dates

FOR 5 GALLONS
60-MINUTE MASH AT 152°F (67°C)
2¾ gallons (10.41 liters) water, plus 5 gallons (18.93 liters) for sparging; 8 pounds (3628.74 grams) Belgian Pilsner malt; 2 pounds (907.19 grams) Belgian Wheat malt; 1.25 pounds (566.99 grams) Caramel 10 malt

60-MINUTE BOIL 1 ounce (28.35 grams) Saaz hops

FERMENT Lambic yeast blend, such as Wyeast Brettanomyces Lambicus; 5 cups (1200 grams) sour cherries, pitted and crushed; 1 cup (340 grams) honey, for bottling

BROOKLYN

BROOKLYN, NY

BREWERY

For us, when it came to beer, writing in the first person plural came naturally. From the start it was a shared adventure in brewing, in traveling, in love, and in starting a business together. There seemed to be only a "we" when it came to our company, our recipes, and our stories. But when it came time for us to write about Brooklyn Brewery, it was different; we had been introduced separately.

For Erica it was her first summer in New York, for an internship at a bridal magazine that no longer exists. She moved to the city knowing no one, set up camp in an NYU dorm, and tracked down friends of friends she had been given as contacts. She made lists of all the things she wanted to do while here, and how to best test out the city she imagined would be her future home after college. And it was on one of those lists that Brooklyn Brewery fell.

Having checked off MOMA, PS1, Katz's Deli, and an outdoor movie in Bryant Park, she went with a group of now friends for a Friday night happy hour at the brewery to sit at picnic tables, order in pizza, and trade tokens for beer, before beer was something she knew how to make.

Stephen's introduction was hazier. Brooklyn Brewery was the brewery named for the borough he grew up in. It's the brewery that picked up the brewing tradition and history he knew his home once had, either from watching PBS specials or from his parents, who, although they don't drink, are full-fledged Brooklynites from the Brooklyn of stoop-sitting, neighbor-knowing sons and daughters of Norwegian immigrants. It's the borough where his mother's father made basement beer during Prohibition.

But when it came to the brewery and the two of us, we kept finding ourselves back there. We went back for special releases and to teach classes on brewing in the kitchen; we went to deliver their first order of co-branded kits and to sign books at a mini-festival. We returned to those same picnic tables following epic bowling staff parties at the nearby lanes to trade more tokens for more beer.

We ate brain tacos (well, Stephen did; Erica did not) with Garrett Oliver at Palo Santo after a festival. Drank an unmarked bottle of a perfect blend. And learned that we shared two more things, an alma mater (Boston University) and major (film).

We sometimes get asked if Brooklyn Brew Shop is related to Brooklyn Brewery, to which we respond, "No. We just share a borough, and a love for beer." But that doesn't mean the connection isn't deep.

BROOKLYN BREWERY PLAYS HOSTS TO A SLEW OF EVENTS THROUGHOUT THE YEAR. CHECK THEIR CALENDAR BEFORE YOU GO.

HINDY'S CHOCOLATE STOUT

7% ABV

60-MINUTE MASH AT 152°F (67°C)

2¼ qt (2.13 l) water, plus 1 gal (3.79 l) for sparging

1.7 lb (771.11 g) English Pale malt

0.21 lb (95.25 g) Chocolate malt

0.11 lb (49.9 g) Black malt

0.11 lb (49.9 g) roasted barley

*All grains should be milled (see page 15).

60-MINUTE BOIL

0.4 oz (11.34 g) Willamette hops

FERMENT

English ale yeast, such as Safale S-04 or Wyeast London Ale III (see note, page 16)

3 Tbsp (63 g) maple syrup, for bottling

WHILE LIVING IN BEIRUT, STEVE HINDY, THE FOUNDER OF BROOKLYN BREWERY, WAS DISAPPOINTED WITH THE CONSIDERABLE LACK OF GOOD BEER, SO HE MADE HIS OWN. HINDY'S CHOCOLATE STOUT STARTED IT ALL FOR THE BREWERY. IT'S SUPER-DARK, RICH, AND UNLIKE ANYTHING YOU COULD HAVE FOUND IN BEIRUT, FOR SURE.

MASH In a medium stockpot, heat 2¼ quarts (2.13 liters) water over high heat to 160°F (70°C). Add all the malts and stir gently. The temperature should reduce to 150°F (66°C) within 1 minute. Turn off the heat. Steep the grains for 60 minutes between 144°F and 152°F (62°C and 67°C). Every 10 minutes, stir and take the temperature. If the grains get too cold, turn the heat to high and stir until the temperature rises to that range, then turn off the heat. With 10 minutes left, in a second medium stockpot heat 1 gallon (3.79 liters) water to 170°F (77°C). After the grains have steeped for 60 minutes, turn the heat to high and stir until the temperature reaches 170°F (77°C). Turn off the heat.

SPARGE Place a fine-mesh strainer over a stockpot and pour the grains into the strainer, reserving the liquid. Pour the 1 gallon (3.79 liters) of 170°F (77°C) water over the grains. Recirculate the collected liquid through the grains once.

BOIL Return the pot with the liquid to the stove and bring to a boil over high heat. When the liquid starts to foam, reduce the heat to a slow rolling boil and add the Willamette hops. Prepare an ice bath by stopping the sink and filling it halfway with water and ice. At the 60-minute mark, turn off the heat. Place the pot in the ice bath and cool to 70°F (21°C), about 30 minutes.

FERMENT Using a funnel and a strainer, pour the liquid into a sanitized fermenter. Add water as needed to fill the jug to the 1-gallon mark. Add the yeast, sanitize your hands, cover the mouth of the jug with one hand, and shake to distribute evenly. Attach a sanitized stopper and tubing to the fermenter and insert the other end of the tubing into a small bowl of sanitizing solution. The solution will begin to bubble as the yeast activates, pushing gas through the tube. Wait 2 to 3 days, until the bubbling has slowed, then replace the tubing system with an airlock. Wait 11 more days, then bottle, using the maple syrup (see page 13 for bottling instructions).

//

SUGGESTED FOOD PAIRINGS Shepherd's Pie, Spent Grain Pizza (page 57)

FOR 5 GALLONS

60-MINUTE MASH AT 152°F (67°C)

2¾ gallons (10.41 liters) water, plus 5 gallons (18.93 liters) for sparging; 8.5 pounds (3855.54 grams) English Pale malt; 1.05 pounds (476.27 grams) Chocolate malt; 0.55 pound (249.48 grams) Black malt; 0.55 pound (249.48 grams) roasted barley

60-MINUTE BOIL 2 ounces (56.7 grams) Willamette hops

FERMENT English ale yeast, such as Safale S-04 or Wyeast London Ale III; 1 cup (340 grams) maple syrup, for bottling

PRETTY THINGS

BEER & ALE PROJECT

CAMBRIDGE, MA

We like breweries. That's probably obvious. But what is it about a brewery that we like the most? Is it the grain mill or the shiny fermenters? It's certainly not the forklifts. Maybe it's getting to sit in the tasting room and chat with the passing brewers, asking "What hops are in this?" or "Were there any spices added to that?" That's quite fun, but when all is said and done, it's the beer that keeps us coming back. It's just that sometimes there isn't a place to go back to.

Pretty Things doesn't have a brewery. This may make them itinerant or gypsy brewers, but ultimately their being transients isn't why we like them. They make good beer. They don't use strange ingredients for the sake of saying they did. What they make is elegant, easy to enjoy, and brewed by people who are easy to love.

"It's important to us to be able to turn everything on its head from time to time without asking permission," says Martha Holley-Paquette, who, along with Dann Paquette, husband and brewer, presides over the

Pretty Things Beer & Ale Project out of Massachusetts.

Given that beer tastes evolve with the passing years, the casual observer might conclude that deciding to brew recipes unseen for more than a century would indicate things being turned on their heads, but that's the basis of Pretty Thing's Once Upon a Time Series, for which they brew recipes based on brew sheets discovered by beer historian Ron Pattinson. Brew sheets are essentially written records of one brewer's brew day–a day often many years in the past. "We like the idea of a mash tun time machine. [The beer] tastes as it did in history, and if that is not to the liking of the modern palate, so be it," says Martha.

And while they may not have a glass-enclosed tasting room with banners of Jack D'Or, their moustached barley grain of a mascot, welcoming you to their world, they do have plenty of history, century by century, packed in every bottle.

"IT'S IMPORTANT TO US TO BE ABLE TO TURN EVERYTHING ON ITS HEAD FROM TIME TO TIME WITHOUT ASKING PERMISSION."

—MARTHA HOLLEY-PAQUETTE, *PRETTY THINGS CO-OWNER*

RON PATTINSON'S ONCE UPON A TIME: 1945 MILD

3% ABV

60-MINUTE MASH, FIRST 30 MINUTES AT 144°F (62°C), REMAINING 30 MINUTES AT 149°F (65°C)

1 qt (0.95 l) water, plus 1 gal (3.79 l) for sparging

0.25 lb (113.4 g) English Mild malt

0.25 lb (113.4 g) English Pale malt

0.25 lb (113.4 g) American 2-row malt

0.11 lb (49.9 g) flaked barley

0.10 lb (45.36 g) Amber malt

0.07 lb (31.75 g) Crystal 55 malt

*All grains should be milled (see page 15).

90-MINUTE BOIL

0.25 oz (7.09 g) Fuggle hops

0.12 lb (54.43 g) Dark Belgian Candi Sugar

FERMENT

English ale yeast, such as Safale S-04 (see note, page 16)

3 Tbsp (63 g) maple syrup, for bottling

WE OFTEN HEAR STORIES IN AMERICA OF THE GREATEST GENERATION: OUR GRANDPARENTS WHO WENT OFF TO FIGHT IN WORLD WAR II AS WELL AS THOSE WHO HELD DOWN THE HOMESTEAD, STRETCHING RATIONS JUST A LITTLE FURTHER. THIS BEER, A RE-CREATION OF A BRITISH MILD FROM 1945, IS THE PRODUCT OF SIX YEARS OF ENGLISH WAR RATIONING. IT'S LOW IN EVERYTHING, INCLUDING HOPS, MALT, AND ALCOHOL. A BEER MADE THE CENTURY PRIOR, IN 1838, BY THE SAME BREWERY UNDER THE SAME NAME, WAS MORE THAN TWICE AS ALCOHOLIC AND MUCH HOPPIER. WE TRY TO KEEP THE RECIPE AS TRUE TO THE ORIGINAL BREW SHEET AS POSSIBLE, WITH THE EXCEPTION OF MAPLE SYRUP FOR BOTTLING, WHICH IS CLEARLY AN EXTRAVAGANCE ON OUR PART.

MASH In a medium stockpot, heat 1 quart (0.95 liter) water over high heat to 155°F (68°C). Add all the malts and stir gently. The temperature should reduce to 144°F (62°C) within 1 minute. Turn off the heat. Steep the grains for 30 minutes at 144°F (62°C). Every 10 minutes, stir and take the temperature. If the grains get too cold, turn the heat to high and stir until the temperature rises, then turn off the heat. After 30 minutes, turn the heat to high and stir until the temperature reaches 149°F (65°C), then turn off the heat. With 10 minutes left, in a second medium stockpot heat 1 gallon (3.79 liters) water to 170°F (77°C). After the grains have steeped for 60 minutes, turn the heat to high and stir until the temperature reaches 170°F (77°C). Turn off the heat.

SPARGE Place a fine-mesh strainer over a stockpot and pour the grains into the strainer, reserving the liquid. Pour the 1 gallon (3.79 liters) of 170°F (77°C) water over the grains. Recirculate the collected liquid through the grains once.

BOIL Return the pot with the liquid to the stove and bring to a boil over high heat. When the liquid starts to foam, reduce the heat to a slow rolling boil. Add the Fuggle hops after 15 minutes. After 80 minutes, prepare an ice bath by stopping the sink and filling it halfway with water and ice. At the 90-minute mark, turn off the heat, add the Dark Belgian Candi Sugar, and stir to dissolve the sugar. Place the pot in the ice bath and cool to 61°F (16°C), 30 to 35 minutes.

FERMENT Using a funnel and a strainer, pour the liquid into a sanitized fermenter. Add water as needed to fill the jug to the 1-gallon mark. Add the yeast, sanitize your hands, cover the mouth of the jug with one hand, and shake to distribute evenly. Attach a sanitized stopper and tubing to the fermenter and insert the other end of the tubing into a small bowl of sanitizing solution. The solution will begin to bubble as the yeast activates, pushing gas through the tube. Wait 2 to 3 days, until the bubbling has slowed, then replace the tubing system with an airlock. Wait 11 more days, then bottle, using the maple syrup (see page 13 for bottling instructions).

//

SUGGESTED FOOD PAIRINGS Salt pork, boiled potatoes, beans

FOR 5 GALLONS

60-MINUTE MASH, FIRST 30 MINUTES AT 144°F (62°C), REMAINING 30 MINUTES AT 149°F (65°C): 5 quarts (4.73 liters) water, plus 5 gallons (18.92 liters) for sparging; 1.25 pounds (566.99 grams) English Mild malt; 1.25 pounds (566.99 grams) English Pale malt; 1.25 pounds (566.99 grams) 2-row malt; 0.55 pound (249.48 grams) flaked barley; 0.50 pound (226.8 grams) Amber malt; 0.35 pound (158.76 grams) Crystal 55 malt

90-MINUTE BOIL 1.25 ounces (28.35 grams) Fuggle hops; 0.6 pound (272.16 grams) Dark Belgian Candi Sugar

FERMENT English ale yeast, such as Safale S-04; 1 cup (340 grams) maple syrup, for bottling

TASTING YESTERDAY'S BEER

The history of beer spans centuries, cultures, and continents, and one of its historians may wade through a wealth of sepia-toned photographs or vintage posters for brands long ago forgotten and come up with little more than the locations of empty brick buildings where breweries once stood.

Little has changed when discussing beer from the past to the present day in the sense that what's in the bottle is what counts most. A story of beer's history goes down better with a full glass, especially one made in the style of another time.

Ron Pattinson, a British beer historian based in Amsterdam, has made it his mission to uncover the tastes of traditional styles and brewing methods across Europe. "There are a lot of things that have been lost. People would be surprised to find out what British beer was like," says Pattinson, who's teamed up with the folks behind Pretty Things Beer & Ale Project out of Cambridge, Massachusetts, to brew re-creations of beers based on recovered historic brew sheets.

Brewers kept brew sheets as they went about making beer, and each act as a recording of one day at a brewery. They list what went into a batch, how long each step took, and note anything worth remembering for the next time. Before computers, brew sheets were how a brewery could ensure some sense of continuity from one batch to the next. They also hold the secrets to re-creating historic beers. "Finding these brew sheets was the only way to know what beer was really like," says Pattinson.

Since a brew sheet is simply a recording of one day's batch, a beer could change over time with evolving tastes or shifting necessities. "A beer sold under one name can become very different over the years. Wartime beers, in particular, are weird. They're more inventive, often using more colored malts to make up for what would otherwise be light and watery."

To try your hand at your own wartime warmer, take a look at the Once Upon a Time: 1945 Mild (page 122).

Next time you begin your brew day by placing your stainless-steel brew pots atop your gas stove and sanitizing your glass thermometer and other small plastic and rubber pieces now indispensable to the modern brewer, think of yesterday's resourceful brewers and what they were able to accomplish with much less. Thanks to Ron Pattinson, you may even be able to taste what they made with far fewer resources than we have today.

"People weren't stupid. For cleaning, they used things like lye and steam, and the beers were in reasonably good condition when they left the brewery. It was up to the publicans to screw them up." Tell this to a brewer today, and you might hear that little has changed.

BEER & BACON MAC & CHEESE

SERVES 4

2 Tbsp (28 g) unsalted butter, plus more for greasing the dish

1 lb (453.59 g) chioccioIe (snail-shaped) or large elbow pasta

2 Tbsp (15.63 g) all-purpose flour

1 cup (0.24 l) buttermilk

1 cup (0.24 l) Bacon Dubbel (page 112) or other dark, flavorful beer

8 oz (28.35 g) aged cheddar, grated

¼ tsp (0.57 g) paprika

Pinch of cayenne

Pinch of grated nutmeg

4 slices bacon, cooked until crisp, then chopped

½ cup (0.12 l) coarsely chopped dried spent grain (see page 56) or panko

IF WE EVER FIND OURSELVES GOING TO BED ON AN EMPTY STOMACH, THIS IS WHAT WE DREAM OF. IT'S A DANGEROUS DISH—TOO TEMPTING FOR SELF-CONTROL TO ENTER THE PICTURE, ESPECIALLY ONCE THE AROMATIC SMOKE OF THE BACON, MALT SWEETNESS OF THE BEER, AND RICHNESS OF THE CHEDDAR THOROUGHLY BLEND AND BEGIN BUBBLING IN YOUR OVEN.

///

1 Preheat the oven to 375°F (190°C). Butter an 8-inch square baking dish.

2 Boil the pasta in heavily salted water until al dente. Drain and set aside.

3 In a saucepan over medium-high heat, melt the butter and whisk in the flour (to make a roux); cook for 1 to 2 minutes until the roux begins to brown. Add the buttermilk and beer, whisking continuously. Add the cheese in three parts, stirring after each addition until the cheese has completely melted. Lower the heat and stir for 5 minutes. Stir in the spices and bacon.

4 Put the pasta in the baking dish and pour the cheese sauce over evenly. Top with the dried spent grain.

5 Bake for 25 minutes or until bubbly and golden brown on top. Let cool slightly before serving.

ABBEY ONION SOUP

SERVES 4

5 large yellow onions, thinly sliced

4 Tbsp (56 g) unsalted butter

1 tsp (4 g) all-purpose flour

3 cups (0.7 l) Bruxelles Black (page 104) or other dark, Belgian abbey-style ale

3 cups (0.7 l) beef stock

2 bay leaves

4 slices crusty bread, for topping

2 cups (226.79 g) grated Gruyère, for topping

WE LOVE THE LAYERS OF FLAVOR DEVELOPED FROM SLOW-COOKING AN ONION SOUP—BUT WE DON'T ALWAYS HAVE THE HOURS TO WAIT FOR IT. SPIKING THE BROTH WITH A NICE DARK ABBEY ALE LIKE OUR BRUXELLES BLACK AND QUICKLY CARAMELIZING THE ONIONS OVER A HIGHER HEAT ARE GREAT CHEATS FOR GETTING THE FULL FLAVOR WITHOUT THE FULL TIME.

//

1 In a large heavy-bottomed pot, cook the onions in the butter over medium-high heat, stirring every 10 minutes until caramelized but not burnt, about 40 minutes. Sprinkle the flour evenly and cook, stirring continuously, for 3 minutes. Add the beer, stock, and bay leaves and bring to a boil while stirring. Reduce the heat, cover, and simmer for 20 minutes.

2 Preheat the broiler.

3 Top the bread slices with the Gruyère, place on a baking sheet, and broil for 2 minutes or until the cheese is bubbly.

4 To serve, place a toast in each bowl. Remove the bay leaves and ladle the soup over the toasted bread.

BEER BEEF JERKY

SERVES 4

2 lb (907.19 g) flank steak

2 cups (0.47 l) Bruxelles Black (page 104) or other dark, Belgian abbey-style ale

½ cup (0.12 l) soy sauce

2 garlic cloves, sliced

2 Tbsp (42.5 g) honey

1 tsp (1.55 g) hot red pepper flakes

½ tsp (1.15 g) cracked black pepper

Juice of ½ lime

NO ROAD TRIP WOULD BE COMPLETE WITHOUT A COMMUNAL BAG OF BEEF JERKY BEING PASSED BETWEEN DRIVER AND PASSENGER. WE'RE PRETTY BIG FANS OF THE STUFF. IT'S GOTTEN US THROUGH LONG DAYS TRAVELING IN THIS COUNTRY AND ABROAD, SO WE WANTED TO MAKE A BEER-SPIKED VERSION OF OUR OWN. WE MARINATED OURS IN OUR BRUXELLES BLACK, BUT ANY SWEET, DARKER BELGIAN ALE WILL DO THE TRICK. CHOOSE THE FATTIER FLANK STEAK CUT FOR ADDED MOISTURE.

//

1 Remove any visible fat from the flank steak, place in a zip-top bag, and freeze for 2 hours to firm up and make slicing easier. Remove the steak from the freezer and thinly slice the meat (against the grain) into long strips.

2 Mix the remaining ingredients in a large bowl. Combine the marinade and sliced steak in a zip-top bag and refrigerate for at least 6 hours and up to 12 hours.

3 Remove the steak strips from the marinade and arrange them in a single layer in a dehydrator. Set the temperature between 160°F and 165°F (71°C and 74°C) and dry for 6 to 8 hours, or until cooked through but not brittle.

4 Store in a zip-top bag or airtight container, refrigerated, for up to 2 weeks.

WINTER

GATHER

friends and family

AND TOAST

• ★ • ⁄⁄⁄⁄⁄⁄⁄⁄⁄⁄⁄⁄⁄ • ★ •

It's during the chilling cold and shortened days of winter when we often need a beer, and the beers we brew are meant for sipping slowly. Our winter beers feature a rich malt character and heartier spices and aromas like those of peppercorn, smoke, rum, and oak. They're the beers that fill our cups until the first sight of spring.

THE BREWERIES
THAT INSPIRED OUR BREWS

**SCHLENKERLA
(BAMBERG, GERMANY)**

SMOKED WHEAT

**ODELL BREWING COMPANY
(FORT COLLINS, CO)**

**OATMEAL RAISIN
COOKIE STOUT**

**BRASSERIE DIEU DU CIEL
(MONTREAL, CANADA)**

PEPPERCORN RYE

**YAZOO BREWING
(NASHVILLE, TN)**

WARRIOR DOUBLE IPA

**LEFT HAND
BREWING COMPANY
(LONGMONT, CO)**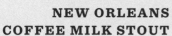

**NEW ORLEANS
COFFEE MILK STOUT**

**EVIL TWIN
(COPENHAGEN, DENMARK /
BROOKLYN, NY)**

**EVIL TWIN'S CHRISTMAS
EVE AT A NEW YORK CITY
HOTEL ROOM**

**GOOSE ISLAND
(CHICAGO, IL)**

RUM BARREL PORTER

PLUS: BAMBERG ONION · WELSH RAREBIT BEER FONDUE · BEER-SOAKED
OVEN FRIES · BLACK PEPPER BEER POUTINE

SCHLENKERLA

BAMBERG, GERMANY

BREWERY

We sometimes hear about bottles of beer being buried on sunken ships or abandoned by arctic expeditions only to be uncovered more than a hundred years later. The liquid inside is still beer. While it might not be the most amazing sip around, it's a little time machine letting us taste and understand the past a bit more clearly.

But there's something to be said for stumbling into the past without the need for a diving bell (or a remotely operated submarine).

There's a cave at the top of a hill in Bavaria filled with tanks of the past, present, and future of beer—or at least of rauchbier, the regional beer of Bamberg, Germany. *Rauchbier* translates to "smoked beer." The barley used in brewing a traditional rauchbier is malted over an open beechwood fire, and it therefore tastes dark, rich, thick, food-like, and above all smoky.

Schlenkerla's brewmaster, Mathias Trum, produces the world's definitive rauchbier as it has been brewed for centuries. "The first special thing is the malt. Schlenkerla, in fact, is not only a brewery; it's also a malt house," says Trum—the sixth generation in his family to helm the brewery that can name its owners going back to 1405. "Nobody would have taken special notice of

that four hundred years ago because it was common-place," he says, but today, with very few exceptions, it's unheard of. Since the Industrial Revolution, barley has been malted in dedicated malt houses and sent to breweries that would previously have needed to do it themselves.

Now Trum tends the last beechwood flame in a city with more breweries than the whole of Ireland— a flame that's been lit and relit time and again, span-ning German unification, two world wars, and the Cold War through today, all while clinging to tradition in a way that makes the history of brewing in the United States seem incredibly brief.

DOWN THE HILL IN THE HEART OF BAMBERG IS THE SCHLENKERLA TAVERN—ONE OF THE MOST MAGICAL PLACES TO DRINK IN EUROPE AND HOME TO THE FRESHEST SCHLEN-KERLA ON TAP ANY-WHERE IN THE WORLD.

SMOKED WHEAT

5% ABV

60-MINUTE MASH AT 152°F (67°C)

2 qt (1.89 l) water, plus 1 gal (3.79 l) for sparging

1 lb (453.59 g) German 2-row malt

0.6 lb (272.16 g) German pale wheat malt

0.2 lb (90.72 g) Special B malt

0.2 lb (90.72 g) Beechwood Smoked malt

*All grains should be milled (see page 15).

60-MINUTE BOIL

0.3 oz (8.5 g) Styrian Golding hops, divided into thirds

FERMENT

German ale yeast, such as Wyeast German Ale (see note, page 16)

3 Tbsp (63 g) maple syrup, for bottling

WE SHOULD START OFF WITH THE DISCLAIMER THAT THIS IS NOT A SCHLENKERLA BEER. THIS BEER DOESN'T HAVE 600 YEARS OF BACKSTORY. IT DOESN'T START WITH MALT-ING BARLEY FOR 36 HOURS OVER AN OPEN FLAME, NOR DOES IT CONSIST OF A NINE-HOUR MASH, BUT WE STILL LOVE IT. IT'S REALLY TASTY. RICH AND MALTY, WITH DEEP SMOKE AND LIGHT BANANA ON THE NOSE, IT'S PERFECT AS BOTH A WINTER WEIZEN AND SUMMER BBQ STAPLE, AND IT'S AS CLOSE AS WE COME TO OWNING A FIREPLACE.

MASH In a medium stockpot, heat 2 quarts (1.89 liters) water over high heat to 160°F (70°C). Add all the malts and stir gently. The temperature should reduce to 150°F (66°C) within 1 minute. Turn off the heat. Steep the grains for 60 minutes between 144°F and 152°F (62°C and 67°C). Every 10 minutes, stir and take the temperature. If the grains get too cold, turn the heat to high and stir until the temperature rises to that range, then turn off the heat. With 10 min-utes left, in a second medium stockpot heat 1 gallon (3.79 liters) water to 170°F (77°C). After the grains have steeped for 60 minutes, turn the heat to high and stir until the temperature reaches 170°F (77°C). Turn off the heat.

SPARGE Place a fine-mesh strainer over a stockpot and pour the grains into the strainer, reserving the liquid. Pour the 1 gallon (3.79 liters) of 170°F (77°C) water over the grains. Recirculate the collected liquid through the grains once.

BOIL Return the pot with the liquid to the stove and bring to a boil over high heat. When the liquid starts to foam, reduce the heat to a slow rolling boil and add one third of the Styrian Golding hops. Add another third of the hops after 30 minutes and the remaining hops after 55 minutes. Prepare an ice bath by stopping the sink and filling it halfway with water and ice. At the 60-minute mark, turn off the heat. Place the pot in the ice bath and cool to 70°F (21°C), about 30 minutes.

FERMENT Using a funnel and a strainer, pour the liquid into a sanitized fermenter. Add water as needed to fill the jug to the 1-gallon mark. Add the yeast, sanitize your hands, cover the mouth of the jug with one hand, and shake to distribute evenly. Attach a sanitized stopper and tubing to the fermenter and insert the other end of the tubing into a small bowl of sanitizing solution. The solution will begin to bubble as the yeast activates, pushing gas through the tube. Wait 2 to 3 days, until the bubbling has slowed, then replace the tubing system with an airlock. Wait 11 more days, then bottle, using the maple syrup (see page 13 for bottling instructions).

//

SUGGESTED FOOD PAIRINGS Bamberg Onion (page 168), Welsh Rarebit Beer Fondue (page 169), white asparagus

FOR 5 GALLONS
60-MINUTE MASH AT 152°F (67°C)
2½ gallons (9.46 liters) water, plus 5 gallons (18.93 liters) for sparging; 5 pounds (2267.96 grams) German 2-row malt; 3 pounds (1360.78 grams) German pale wheat malt; 1 pound (453.59 grams) Special B malt; 1 pound (453.59 grams) Beechwood Smoked malt

60-MINUTE BOIL 1.5 ounces (42.52 grams) Styrian Golding hops, divided into thirds

FERMENT German ale yeast, such as Wyeast German Ale; 1 cup (340 grams) maple syrup, for bottling

BRASSERIE DIEU DU CIEL

BREWERY

MONTREAL, CANADA

Jean-François and his business partner, Stéphane, were going to be microbiologists. That is, until they quit their postgraduate work to become brewers–microbiologists in a different sense. Yeast soon became their microsubject of choice, and Dieu du Ciel became their laboratory.

Even though Dieu du Ciel's roots are scientific, its beers are clearly inspired by food. Maybe because Jean-François started brewing with a strainer in his kitchen, his beers are more closely tied to the table. The ingredients change from beer to beer and season to season.

The Dieu du Ciel brewpub in Montreal, where the pair have been brewing since 1998, is arguably the heart of Canada's craft beer scene. It is here that their Route des épices–a rye beer brewed with peppercorns that has us craving steak with every sip–was born in 2002. It is also where they created Aphrodisiaque, their vanilla and cocoa stout that begs for a scoop of rich French vanilla ice cream either next to or dropped right inside, and Rosée d'hibiscus, which is light, wheat filled, and fragrant.

And it is at the brewpub where friends gather on the outside patio and compare pints of the Solstice d'été aux mangues (mango summer solstice) and ogle the tanks inside marked with collaborations and new variations to come.

Our favorite way to experience Montreal is on bike. The city's bike share (BIXI) has a stop right outside of the Dieu du Ciel brewpub as well as a bunch of other fantastic craft beer destinations.

THE DIEU DU CIEL BREWPUB IS LOCATED IN LE PLATEAU—A HIP NEIGHBORHOOD FILLED WITH GREAT BARS AND RESTAURANTS.

PEPPERCORN RYE

6.25% ABV

60-MINUTE MASH AT 152°F (67°C)

2½ qt (2.37 l) water, plus 1 gal (3.79 l) for sparging

1 lb (453.59 g) Maris Otter malt

0.6 lb (272.16 g) Munich malt

0.5 lb (226.8 g) Rye malt

0.3 lb (136.08 g) Aromatic malt

0.1 lb (45.36 g) Cara-Pils malt

*All grains should be milled (see page 15).

60-MINUTE BOIL

0.3 oz (8.5 g) Challenger hops, divided in half

2 Tbsp (12.5 g) whole black peppercorns

0.24 oz (6.8 g) Willamette hops, divided in half

FERMENT

Belgian ale yeast, such as Safbrew T-58 (see note, page 16)

3 Tbsp (63 g) honey, for bottling

ONE OF OUR FIRST TWO O'CLOCK TASTINGS WITH OUR STAFF CONSISTED OF EIGHT BEERS FROM BRASSERIE DIEU DU CIEL. IT WAS THE LARGEST NUMBER OF BEERS FROM A SINGLE BREWERY WE HAD TAKEN ON IN A TASTING, AND WE WERE ASTOUNDED THAT WE REALLY LIKED EVERY SINGLE ONE. WE WERE PARTICULARLY SMITTEN WITH THE BLACK PEPPER–SPIKED ROUTE DES ÉPICES, WHICH CAN'T BE BEAT AS THE PERFECT RED-MEAT COMPANION. WHEN WE WENT TO CREATE OUR OWN STEAK-WORTHY TRANSLATION, WE PAIRED WARMING RYE MALT AND EARTHY HOPS AND FINISHED WITH A BIG PEPPERCORN BITE.

//

MASH In a medium stockpot, heat 2½ quarts (2.37 liters) water over high heat to 160°F (70°C). Add all the malts and stir gently. The temperature should reduce to 150°F (66°C) within 1 minute. Turn off the heat. Steep the grains for 60 minutes between 144°F and 152°F (62°C and 67°C). Every 10 minutes, stir and take the temperature. If the grains get too cold, turn the heat to high and stir until the temperature rises to that range, then turn off the heat. With 10 minutes left, in a second medium stockpot heat 1 gallon (3.79 liters) water to 170°F (77°C). After the grains have steeped for 60 minutes, turn the heat to high and stir until the temperature reaches 170°F (77°C). Turn off the heat.

SPARGE Place a fine-mesh strainer over a stock-pot and pour the grains into the strainer, reserving the liquid. Pour the 1 gallon (3.79 liters) of 170°F (77°C) water over the grains. Recirculate the collected liquid through the grains once.

BOIL Return the pot with the liquid to the stove and bring to a boil over high heat. When the liquid starts to foam, reduce the heat to a slow rolling boil and add half of the Challenger hops. Add the peppercorns and remaining Challenger hops after 30 minutes. Add half of the Willamette hops after 50 minutes. Prepare an ice bath by stopping the sink and filling it halfway with water and ice. At the 60-minute mark, turn off the heat and add the remaining Willamette hops. Place the pot in the ice bath and cool to 70°F (21°C), about 30 minutes.

FERMENT Using a funnel and a strainer, pour the liquid into a sanitized fermenter. Add water as needed to fill the jug to the 1-gallon mark. Add the yeast, sanitize your hands, cover the mouth of the jug with one hand, and shake to distribute evenly. Attach a sanitized stopper and tubing to the fermenter and insert the other end of the tubing into a small bowl of sanitizing solution. The solution will begin to bubble as the yeast activates, pushing gas through the tube. Wait 2 to 3 days, until the bubbling has slowed, then replace the tubing system with an airlock. Wait 11 more days, then bottle, using the honey (see page 13 for bottling instructions).

SUGGESTED FOOD PAIRINGS Beer-Soaked Oven Fries (page 170), Black Pepper Beer Poutine (page 171), bone-in steak

FOR 5 GALLONS
60-MINUTE MASH AT 152°F (67°C)
3¼ gallons (12.3 liters) water, plus 4 gallons (15.14 liters) for sparging; 5 pounds (2267.96 grams) Maris Otter malt; 3 pounds (1360.78 grams) Munich malt; 2.5 pounds (1133.98 grams) Rye malt; 1.5 pounds (680.39 grams) Aromatic malt; 0.5 pound (226.8 grams) Cara-Pils malt

60-MINUTE BOIL
1.5 ounces (42.5 grams) Challenger hops, divided in half; ⅔ cup (62.5 grams) whole black peppercorns; 1.2 ounces (34 grams) Willamette hops, divided in half

FERMENT Belgian ale yeast, such as Safbrew T-58; 1 cup (340 grams) honey, for bottling

LEFT HAND BREWING COMPANY

LONGMONT, CO

BREWERY

Making beer at home—once ubiquitous, then outlawed, then legalized again in 1979—took some time to regain its rightful place in homes across the United States. Some places, however, reclaimed the brewing tradition a lot quicker than others. The early epicenter for craft beer in the kitchen was Colorado. Good water, no shortage of space, and enthusiastic brewers helped shake the state's atrophied beer culture, while much of the country slowly recovered from Prohibition and lingering midcentury food tastes.

One thing is certain on any trip to Colorado: You'll drink good beer. Great beer, really. And lots of it. Pints you've never had before from breweries you may never see again after you return home. Good beer is everywhere, and it's glorious, and it typically makes for quite a fun trip.

This wouldn't be possible without the pioneering breweries that opened shop, converted old machine shops and warehouses, or, in the case of the Left Hand Brewing Company, turned an old meatpacking plant into a fully functional brewery pumping out some of the most interesting and groundbreaking beers this side of the Atlantic.

Left Hand makes some weird beers, or at least they sounded weird when we first heard of them near the early stages of our beer-making days. We thought putting milk (or at least milk sugar) in beer was quite peculiar, but their Milk Stout has arguably defined the category for the country at large. It's delicious, and we're hard-pressed not to draw inspiration from it whenever we're brewing one ourselves. Adding ginger to a beer also used to be an anomaly, let alone bottling it en masse in six-packs, but they did it with their Good Juju. They've made a specialty over the years of taking the strangeness out of the strange, serving it up, and bringing Colorado along with the rest of the world into beer's future.

ONE THING IS CERTAIN ON ANY TRIP TO COLORADO: YOU'LL DRINK GOOD BEER.

NEW ORLEANS COFFEE MILK STOUT

7.5% ABV

60-MINUTE MASH AT 152°F (67°C)

2½ qt (2.37 l) water, plus 1 gal (3.79 l) for sparging

1.5 lb (680.39 g) Pale malt

0.4 lb (181.44 g) Caramel 40 malt

0.2 lb (90.72 g) Caramel 120 malt

0.2 lb (90.72 g) Chocolate malt

0.1 lb (45.36 g) Black malt

0.1 lb (45.36 g) roasted barley

0.1 lb (45.36 g) flaked oats

*All grains should be milled (see page 15).

60-MINUTE BOIL

0.05 oz (1.42 g) Magnum hops

0.25 oz (7.09 g) Progress hops, divided into fifths

0.2 lb (90.72 g) lactose sugar

¼ cup (20 g) coffee beans, crushed

¼ cup (20 g) roasted chicory root (see Sources, page 173)

FERMENT

Belgian ale yeast, such as Safale S-33 (see note, page 16)

3 Tbsp (63 g) maple syrup, for bottling

LEFT HAND SAYS ADDING MILK SUGAR (LACTOSE) TO BEER IS LIKE ADDING CREAM TO COFFEE. BEER TYPICALLY GETS ALL ITS SUGARS FROM BARLEY (MALTOSE), BUT LACTOSE IS A LITTLE DIFFERENT. TYPICALLY, SUGAR BECOMES ALCOHOL. LACTOSE, HOWEVER, DOESN'T PLAY BY THOSE RULES. IT'S MOSTLY UNFERMENTABLE, SO ITS SWEETNESS, ALTHOUGH MILD, IS PRESERVED IN THE END PRODUCT. PAIRED WITH FLAKED OATS FOR A SILKY BODY, THE LACTOSE LENDS A REAL CREAMINESS TO A HEAVILY ROASTED STOUT THAT REMINDS US OF A NEW ORLEANS–STYLE COFFEE. WE ADD IN CHICORY ROOT (A TRADI-TIONAL INGREDIENT IN NOLA COFFEE) TO BUMP UP THE BEER'S SWEET BUT DEEP ROASTINESS.

//

MASH In a medium stockpot, heat 2½ quarts (2.37 liters) water over high heat to 160°F (70°C). Add all the grains and stir gently. The temperature should reduce to 150°F (66°C) within 1 minute. Turn off the heat. Steep the grains for 60 minutes between 144°F and 152°F (62°C and 67°C). Every 10 minutes, stir and take the temperature. If the grains get too cold, turn the heat to high and stir until the temperature rises to that range, then turn off the heat. With 10 minutes left, in a second medium stockpot heat 1 gallon (3.79 liters) water to 170°F (77°C). After the grains have steeped for 60 minutes, turn the heat to high and stir until the temperature reaches 170°F (77°C). Turn off the heat.

SPARGE Place a fine-mesh strainer over a stock-pot and pour the grains into the strainer, reserving the liquid. Pour the 1 gallon (3.79 liters) of 170°F (77°C) water over the grains. Recirculate the collected liquid through the grains once.

BOIL Return the pot with the liquid to the stove and bring to a boil over high heat. When the liquid starts to foam, reduce the heat to a slow rolling boil and add the Magnum hops. Add two fifths of the Progress hops after 20 minutes. Add one fifth of the Progress hops after 40 minutes and another fifth after 50 minutes. Prepare an ice bath by stopping the sink and filling it halfway with water and ice. At the 60-minute mark, turn off the heat and add the remaining fifth of the Progress hops, the lactose sugar, coffee, and chicory; stir to dissolve the sugar. Place the pot in the ice bath and cool to 70°F (21°C), about 30 minutes.

FERMENT Using a funnel and a strainer, pour the liquid into a sanitized fermenter. Add water as needed to fill the jug to the 1-gallon mark. Add the yeast, sanitize your hands, cover the mouth of the jug with one hand, and shake to distribute evenly. Attach a sanitized stopper and tubing to the fermenter and insert the other end of the tubing into a small bowl of sanitizing solution. The solution will begin to bubble as the yeast activates, pushing gas through the tube. Wait 2 to 3 days, until the bubbling has slowed, then replace the tubing system with an airlock. Wait 11 more days, then bottle, using the maple syrup (see page 13 for bottling instructions).

SUGGESTED FOOD PAIRINGS Mole, affogato, stout milkshake

FOR 5 GALLONS

60-MINUTE MASH AT 152°F (67°C)

3¼ gallons (12.3 liters) water, plus 4 gallons (15.14 liters) for sparging; 7.5 pounds (3401.94 grams) Pale malt; 2 pounds (907.19 grams) Caramel 40 malt; 1 pound (453.59 grams) Caramel 120 malt; 1 pound (453.59 grams) Chocolate malt; 0.5 pound (226.8 grams) Black malt; 0.5 pound (226.8 grams) roasted barley; 0.5 pound (226.8 grams) flaked oats

60-MINUTE BOIL

0.25 ounce (7.08 grams) Magnum hops; 1.25 ounce (35.44 grams) Progress hops, divided into fifths; 1 pound (453.59 grams) lactose sugar; 1¼ cups (100 grams) coffee beans, crushed; 1¼ cups (100 grams) roasted chicory root

FERMENT Belgian ale yeast, such as Safale S-33; 1 cup (340 grams) maple syrup, for bottling

GOOSE ISLAND

CHICAGO, IL

BREWERY

If you ask any beer drinker what his or her favorite Goose Island beer is, you're bound to get different answers. The brewery seems to whip up something for everyone.

Those who prefer downright tasty beer made simply with malt, hops, and yeast trust their line of Classic Ales, ubiquitous in Chicago and beyond, while lovers of intensely dark, charred, burningly alcoholic beers go wild for their Bourbon County Stout, an imperial stout aged in bourbon barrels. Fans will cellar Goose Island bottles for years and exchange tasting notes on various vintages over the Internet. Upon visiting we walked through the barrel warehouse to a large room lined floor to ceiling and wall to wall with barrels in a way that made it appear as if they were locking away government secrets.

All the Goose Island beers—whether light, dark, easy-drinking, complex, sweet, bitter, or tart—have one common thread: They should be consumed with food . . . preferably good food. Be it with a burger (Classic), a cheese plate (Vintage), or an incredibly decadent slice of chocolate cake (Bourbon County), there's a strong chance Goose Island brews something to serve alongside whatever food you crave.

Goose Island's barrel-aging program is massive. While other breweries may have a pet project of eight or so barrels (each previously used to store something different) lined up against one wall, Goose Island has entire warehouses dedicated to barrel-aging beer.

GOOSE ISLAND HAS ENTIRE WAREHOUSES DEDICATED TO BARREL-AGING BEER.

RUM BARREL PORTER

6% ABV

PREP

0.75 oz (21 g) dark oak chips (available at brewing supply stores; see Sources, page 173)

⅓ cup (0.08 l) dark rum

60-MINUTE MASH AT 152°F (67°C)

2½ qt (2.37 l) water, plus 1 gal (3.79 l) for sparging

1.5 lb (680.39 g) Pale malt

0.4 lb (181.44 g) Caramel 60 malt

0.25 lb (113.4 g) Special B malt

0.1 lb (45.36 g) Chocolate malt

0.1 lb (45.36 g) Black malt

*All grains should be milled (see page 15).

60-MINUTE BOIL

0.2 oz (5.67 g) Centennial hops, divided in half

0.2 oz (5.67 g) Willamette hops, divided in half

FERMENT

Belgian ale yeast, such as Safale S-33 (see note, page 16)

3 Tbsp (63 g) maple syrup, for bottling

PORTERS (THE BEER STYLE) AND RUM SHARE A LONG NAUTI-CAL HISTORY, BUT LIKE SHIPS PASSING IN THE NIGHT, THEIR COLLIDING IS A VERY RARE OCCURRENCE. WE CHALK IT UP IN LARGE PART TO GEOGRAPHY. PORTERS ARE COLD-WEATHER BEERS. THEY'RE BEST SERVED TO THOSE BUNDLED UP. DARK, WARMING, AND RICH, THEY'RE OUR GO-TO WINTER BEERS. RUM, ON THE OTHER HAND, IS TROPICAL. IT'S LIGHT AND FESTIVE. A DARK AND STORMY ISN'T EVEN ALL THAT DARK OR STORMY. RUM DOES, HOWEVER, LEND ITSELF NICELY TO RICHER PURPOSES (THINK CAKE OR ANY COCKTAIL WITH A TINY UMBRELLA)—AND NOW BEER.

///

PREP The day before brewing, in a shallow tray, soak the oak chips in the rum at room temperature. Keep covered overnight.

MASH In a medium stockpot, heat 2½ quarts (2.37 liters) water over high heat to 160°F (70°C). Add all the malts and stir gently. The temperature should reduce to 150°F (66°C) within 1 minute. Turn off the heat. Steep the grains for 60 minutes between 144°F and 152°F (62°C and 67°C). Every 10 minutes, stir and take the temperature. If the grains get too cold, turn the heat to high and stir until the temperature rises to that range, then turn off the heat. With 10 minutes left, in a second medium stockpot heat 1 gallon (3.79 liters) water to 170°F (77°C). After the grains have steeped for 60 minutes, turn the heat to high and stir until the temperature reaches 170°F (77°C). Turn off the heat.

SPARGE Place a fine-mesh strainer over a stock-pot and pour the grains into the strainer, reserving the liquid. Pour the 1 gallon (3.79 liters) of 170°F (77°C) water over the grains. Recirculate the collected liquid through the grains once.

BOIL Return the pot with the liquid to the stove and bring to a boil over high heat. When the liquid starts to foam, reduce the heat to a slow rolling boil and add half of the Centennial hops. Add the remaining Centennial hops after 30 minutes. Add half of the Willamette hops after 50 minutes. Prepare an ice bath by stopping the sink and filling it halfway with water and ice. At the 60-minute mark, turn off the heat and add the remaining Willamette hops and the oak chips and rum. Place the pot in the ice bath and cool to 70°F (21°C), about 30 minutes.

FERMENT Using a funnel and a strainer, pour the liquid into a sanitized fermenter. Add water as needed to fill the jug to the 1-gallon mark. Add the yeast, sanitize your hands, cover the mouth of the jug with one hand, and shake to distribute evenly. Attach a sanitized stopper and tubing to the fermenter and insert the other end of the tubing into a small bowl of sanitizing solution. The solution will begin to bubble as the yeast activates, pushing gas through the tube. Wait 2 to 3 days, until the bubbling has slowed, then replace the tubing system with an airlock. Wait 11 more days, then bottle, using the maple syrup (see page 13 for bottling instructions).

//

SUGGESTED FOOD PAIRINGS Jerk chicken, sweet plantains, rum cake

FOR 5 GALLONS

PREP 3.75 ounces (106.31 grams) dark oak chips; 1⅔ cups (0.4 liter) dark rum

60-MINUTE MASH AT 152°F (67°C)
3¼ gallons (12.3 liters) water, plus 4 gallons (15.14 liters) for sparging; 7.5 pounds (3401.94 grams) Pale malt; 2 pounds (907.19 grams) Caramel 60 malt; 1.25 pounds (567 grams) Special B malt; 0.5 pound (226.8 grams) Chocolate malt; 0.5 pound (226.8 grams) Black malt

60-MINUTE BOIL 1 ounce (28.35 grams) Centennial hops, divided in half; 1 ounce (28.35 grams) Willamette hops, divided in half

FERMENT Belgian ale yeast, such as Safale S-33; 1 cup (340 grams) maple syrup, for bottling

ODELL BREWING COMPANY

FORT COLLINS, CO

BREWERY

Snowy winters in New York City are quite pretty . . . for about a day. On day two, the snow grays and the icy puddles find their inevitable entry point to galoshes citywide.

Winter in the mountains, however, feels different. Most cars don a ski rack, and instead of heading for sandy beaches and warmer pastures, great processions make their way toward white, pillowy, manicured mountain snow. Here, an entire population sits upon chairlifts only to gracefully descend the green circle, blue square, and black diamond slopes while the newly initiated stumble down the bunny slopes with skis positioned in tight-kneed pizza-wedges.

However, the most apparent trait of winter in the mountains is that it's cold, and the cold lasts quite a while. When a brewery is able to replace the heavily churning air compressor powering its cold-storage warehouse with a fan that simply brings in the outside air for a significant portion of the year, you know it's cold.

And when it's cold, a beer that warms you up is ideal—whether you're in a Brooklyn loft or the Odell Brewing Company's tasting room in Fort Collins, Colorado. Odell makes some big beers. Some are oak aged in their barrel room, others simply loaded with mounds of fresh ingredients. They're high in alcohol, in bitterness, in malt character, and in body. Perfect for post-slope sipping by the fire.

Brendan McGivney, Odell's director of production, speaks with the same degree of pride about every kilowatt saved as he does their newest seasonal release or their most recent barrel experiment. Sustainability in brewing is as important as the beer they produce.

THE BEST PLACE TO SAMPLE ODELL'S BEER IS THEIR TASTING ROOM. GRAB A FLIGHT (OR TWO) ON YOUR NEXT VISIT.

OATMEAL RAISIN COOKIE STOUT

5.1% ABV

60-MINUTE MASH AT 152°F (67°C)

2 qt (1.89 l) water, plus 1 gal (3.79 l) for sparging

1 lb (453.59 g) American 2-row malt

0.3 lb (136.08 g) Chocolate malt

0.3 lb (136.08 g) flaked oats

0.2 lb (90.72 g) Caramel 60 malt

*All grains should be milled (see page 15).

60-MINUTE BOIL

0.3 oz (8.5 g) East Kent Golding hops, divided into thirds

1 cinnamon stick

¼ cup (55 g) packed light brown sugar

¼ cup (30 g) raisins

FERMENT

Belgian ale yeast, such as Safale S-33 (see note, page 16)

3 Tbsp (63 g) maple syrup, for bottling

FEW THINGS COMPARE TO COMING IN ON A COLD DAY, KICKING OFF YOUR BOOTS, AND BEING GREETED BY A FRESH TRAY OF WARM COOKIES. THIS IS THE STUFF TWELVE-YEAR-OLDS DREAM OF, BUT WHETHER WE LIKE IT OR NOT, EVERYONE GETS OLDER. OUR WAY OF FIGHTING BACK THIS WINTER IS BY CAPTURING THAT SAME FEELING OF CHILDHOOD WHILE MAKING IT A LITTLE MORE APPROPRIATE FOR THE GROWN-UPS WE'VE BEGRUDGINGLY BECOME. RICH, CREAMY, AND HINTING OF SPICE, OUR OATMEAL RAISIN COOKIE STOUT IS BREWED WITH CINNAMON, BROWN SUGAR, AND RAISINS, MAKING FOR A COLD PINT OF WARM COOKIES.

MASH In a medium stockpot, heat 2 quarts (1.89 liters) water over high heat to 160°F (70°C). Add all the malts and the oats and stir gently. The temperature should reduce to 150°F (66°C) within 1 minute. Turn off the heat. Steep the grains for 60 minutes between 144°F and 152°F (62°C and 67°C). Every 10 minutes, stir and take the temperature. If the grains get too cold, turn the heat to high and stir until the temperature rises to that range, then turn off the heat. With 10 minutes left, in a second medium stockpot heat 1 gallon (3.79 liters) water to 170°F (77°C). After the grains have steeped for 60 minutes, turn the heat to high and stir until the temperature reaches 170°F (77°C). Turn off the heat.

SPARGE Place a fine-mesh strainer over a stock-pot and pour the grains into the strainer, reserving the liquid. Pour the 1 gallon (3.79 liters) of 170°F (77°C) water over the grains. Recirculate the collected liquid through the grains once.

BOIL Return the pot with the liquid to the stove and bring to a boil over high heat. When the liquid starts to foam, reduce the heat to a slow rolling boil and add two thirds of the East Kent Golding hops. Add the cinnamon stick after 30 minutes and the remaining third East Kent Golding hops after 45 minutes. Prepare an ice bath by stopping the sink and filling it halfway with water and ice. At the 60-minute mark, turn off the heat, add the raisins and brown sugar, and stir to dissolve the sugar. Place the pot in the ice bath and cool to 70°F (21°C), about 30 minutes.

FERMENT Using a funnel and a strainer, pour the liquid into a sanitized fermenter. Add water as needed to fill the jug to the 1-gallon mark. Add the yeast, sanitize your hands, cover the mouth of the jug with one hand, and shake to distribute evenly. Attach a sanitized stopper and tubing to the fermenter and insert the other end of the tubing into a small bowl of sanitizing solution. The solution will begin to bubble as the yeast activates, pushing gas through the tube. Wait 2 to 3 days, until the bubbling has slowed, then replace the tubing system with an airlock. Wait 11 more days, then bottle, using the maple syrup (see page 13 for bottling instructions).

//

SUGGESTED FOOD PAIRINGS Oatmeal raisin cookies, cinnamon rolls, crème brûlée

FOR 5 GALLONS
60-MINUTE MASH AT 152°F (67°C)
2½ gallons (9.46 liters) water, plus 5 gallons (18.93 liters) for sparging; 5 pounds (2267.96 grams) American 2-row malt; 1.5 pounds (680.39 grams) Chocolate malt; 1.5 pounds (680.39 grams) flaked oats; 1 pound (453.59 grams) Caramel 60 malt

60-MINUTE BOIL 1.5 ounces (42.52 grams) East Kent Golding hops; 5 cinnamon sticks; 1¼ cups (175 grams) packed light brown sugar; 1¼ cups (190 grams) raisins

FERMENT Belgian ale yeast, such as Safale S-33; 1 cup (340 grams) maple syrup, for bottling

YAZOO BREWING

BREWERY

NASHVILLE, TN

From the moment you get to Nashville, two things are certain: First, you realize this is indeed Music City. Live bands seemingly play everywhere (even at the airport). And second, Yazoo Brewing's Dos Perros dominates the local taps.

Founder and brewer Linus Hall started brewing with a beer kit he ordered from the back of a *Rolling Stone* magazine in 1993 and, with a decade of batches under his belt, opened Yazoo Brewing's doors in 2003.

The brewery has since relocated to the ever-hip Gulch neighborhood; on Saturdays a food truck sits outside and the line for the bar snakes around the room like a famed BBQ joint. The communal tables are packed with people sharing pints and samplers of both Yazoo classics (like the Dos Perros) and taps that rotate with the seasons.

Hop Project, one of the most popular offerings at Yazoo, is a chameleon of a beer. The exact blend of hops changes every time it's brewed, so no matter how many times you order it, you'll never drink the same beer twice. Next week's pint may be super-grapefruit-citrusy while today's may take you on a beer-guided trip to a pine forest.

While city planning remains a mystery to us, it's an obvious notion that sometimes certain types of businesses begin to pop up near another. In New York, we have the flower district and the diamond district. And while the Gulch is far from saturated in beer, it's quickly rising to become Nashville's—if not Tennessee's—go-to beer destination.

Just a couple blocks away you'll find Jackalope Brewing. Only a few years old and two thirds female-owned, they're the epitome of happy-go-lucky craft-beer optimism. And while the staff might look like a bunch of kids (we're not ones to judge), they brew up some expertly crafted and highly balanced beers with namesakes fit for a mythical petting zoo (see their Leghorn Rye IPA or Rompo, which apparently has the head of a rabbit, ears of a human, arms of a badger, and the legs of a bear).

And with such great neighbors, there's no need to choose favorites.

WARRIOR DOUBLE IPA

7% ABV

60-MINUTE MASH AT 152°F (67°C)

3 qt (2.83 l) water, plus 1 gal (3.79 l) for sparging

2.3 lb (1043.26 g) Pale malt

0.4 lb (181.44 g) CaraRed malt

0.2 lb (90.72 g) Munich malt

*All grains should be milled (see page 15).

75-MINUTE BOIL

0.4 oz (11.34 g) Warrior hops, divided into quarters

FERMENT

American ale yeast, such as Safale S-05 (see note, page 16)

3 Tbsp (63 g) honey, for bottling

DOZENS OF VARIETIES OF HOPS GROW IN THE WILD. LIKE TULIPS, TOMATOES, AND MOST OTHER PLANTS CULTIVATED FOR EATING OR ADMIRING FROM AFAR, THEY'RE BRED ACROSS THE WORLD FOR A WIDE RANGE OF CHARACTERISTICS. THE YAKIMA CHIEF RANCHES IN WASHINGTON FIRST DEVELOPED THE SPECIFIC TYPE OF HOP WE'RE USING IN THIS DOUBLE IPA. THEY NAMED THEIR NEW HOP WARRIOR, MOST LIKELY FOR ITS ABILITY TO PROVIDE AGGRESSIVELY HIGH LEVELS OF CLEAN BITTERNESS TO A BEER AND NOT BECAUSE OF ITS RELATIVELY HIGH RESISTANCE TO POWDERY MILDEW. OUR PERSONAL HOP PROJECT IS A BEER THAT IS CLEAN, BALANCED, BITTER, FLORAL, AND CITRUSY.

//

MASH In a medium stockpot, heat 3 quarts (2.83 liters) water over high heat to 160°F (70°C). Add all the malts and stir gently. The temperature should reduce to 150°F (66°C) within 1 minute. Turn off the heat. Steep the grains for 60 minutes between 144°F and 152°F (62°C and 67°C). Every 10 minutes, stir and take the temperature. If the grains get too cold, turn the heat to high and stir until the temperature rises to that range, then turn off the heat. With 10 minutes left, in a second medium stockpot heat 1 gallon (3.79 liters) water to 170°F (77°C). After the grains have steeped for 60 minutes, turn the heat to high and stir until the temperature reaches 170°F (77°C). Turn off the heat.

SPARGE Place a fine-mesh strainer over a stock-pot and pour the grains into the strainer, reserving the liquid. Pour the 1 gallon (3.79 liters) of 170°F (77°C) water over the grains. Recirculate the collected liquid through the grains once.

BOIL Return the pot with the liquid to the stove and bring to a boil over high heat. When the liquid starts to foam, reduce the heat to a slow rolling boil. Add a quarter of the Warrior hops after 15 minutes, 45 minutes, and 65 minutes. Prepare an ice bath by stopping the sink and filling it halfway with water and ice. At the 75-minute mark, turn off the heat and add the remaining quarter Warrior hops. Place the pot in the ice bath and cool to 70°F (21°C), about 30 minutes.

FERMENT Using a funnel and a strainer, pour the liquid into a sanitized fermenter. Add water as needed to fill the jug to the 1-gallon mark. Add the yeast, sanitize your hands, cover the mouth of the jug with one hand, and shake to distribute evenly. Attach a sanitized stopper and tubing to the fermenter and insert the other end of the tubing into a small bowl of sanitizing solution. The solution will begin to bubble as the yeast activates, pushing gas through the tube. Wait 2 to 3 days, until the bubbling has slowed, then replace the tubing system with an airlock. Wait 11 more days, then bottle, using the honey (see page 13 for bottling instructions).

SUGGESTED FOOD PAIRINGS Nashville-style hot chicken, andouille sausage, oven-fried potatoes

FOR 5 GALLONS

60-MINUTE MASH AT 152°F (67°C)
3¾ gallons (14.2 liters) water, plus 5 gallons (15.14 liters) for sparging; 11.5 pounds (5216.31 grams) Pale malt; 2 pounds (907.19 grams) CaraRed malt; 1 pound (453.59 grams) Munich malt

75-MINUTE BOIL 2 ounces (56.7 grams) Warrior hops, divided into quarters

FERMENT American ale yeast, such as Safale S-05; 1 cup (340 grams) honey, for bottling

EVIL TWIN

COPENHAGEN, DENMARK / BROOKLYN, NY

BREWERY

In most cases, a brewery making beer on multiple continents and shipping slick, beautifully designed cans around the world would be thought of as a multinational juggernaut of a company—not a husband-and-wife team in a Brooklyn apartment with two children. But in the case of Evil Twin, the transcontinental contract brewing operation started by the Danish-born Jeppe Jarnit-Bjergsø, cans of beer are the only physical evidence that a brewery even exists.

Evil Twin doesn't own a mash tun, any tall, shiny fermenters, or a building to put them in. The only brewing equipment they own can fit on a stove.

"I've been brewing at home for ten years," says Jeppe, who first got into beer professionally in 2005 when opening Ølbutikken (Danish for the Beer Shop) in Copenhagen. From there, Jeppe began importing and distributing beers across Europe before making the leap across the Atlantic. When asked about his brewing education, he says, "I'm a schoolteacher." Aside from that, his beer education came from the kitchen and talking with brewers who knew of his shop.

Jeppe brewed a few batches with well-known European breweries before starting to partner with relatively unknown brewers stateside, where Evil Twin now releases more than one new beer per month, almost all of which jump to the top of any number of "Best Beer" lists. "I didn't want to build Evil Twin on other people's success and have people say that the only reason I made it is because I can brew with amazing people."

Ensuring its place on the dinner table, Evil Twin brews house beers for Denmark's NOMA, which many consider the world's preeminent restaurant and which opened TØRST and Luksus, a craft beer bar and the restaurant inside it (that's helmed by a Momofuku alum) located in Greenpoint, Brooklyn. They also brew for Pok Pok, a stunning restaurant transplant to Brooklyn by way of Portland, Oregon.

"I make beers for myself and what I like," says Jeppe. It turns out beer lovers worldwide agree.

> "I MAKE BEERS FOR MYSELF AND WHAT I LIKE."
>
> —JEPPE JARNIT-BJERGSØ,
> *EVIL TWIN FOUNDER*

EVIL TWIN'S CHRISTMAS EVE AT A NEW YORK CITY HOTEL ROOM

10% ABV

60-MINUTE MASH AT 152°F (67°C)

3 1/2 quarts (3.31 liters) water, plus 1 gallon (3.79 liters) for sparging

2.26 pounds (1025.12 grams) German Pilsner malt

0.31 pound (140.61 grams) Caramel 120 malt

0.22 pound (99.79 grams) Chocolate malt

0.21 pound (95.25 grams) Special B malt

0.21 pound (95.26 grams) Beechwood Smoked malt

0.21 pound (95.26 grams) roasted barley

*All grains should be milled (see page 15).

90-MINUTE BOIL

0.16 ounce (4.54 grams) Magnum hops

0.14 ounce (3.97 grams) Chinook hops

0.28 ounce (7.94 grams) Cascade hops

0.28 ounce (7.94 grams) Styrian Golding hops

THIS BEER COMES DIRECTLY FROM JEPPE JARNIT-BJERGSØ OF EVIL TWIN. SCANDANAVIANS TAKE CHRISTMAS AND CHRIST-MAS BEERS SPECIFICALLY VERY SERIOUSLY. "WHEN WE GET INTO THE END OF OCTOBER, PEOPLE STOP BUYING BEERS EXCEPT FOR CHRISTMAS BEER," SAYS JEPPE. "I HATE IT. I HATE CHRISTMAS BEER." SO FOR THIS HOLIDAY ALE, WE SKIP THE CINNAMON AND NUTMEG AND OPT INSTEAD FOR A BIG, HEAVY, HIGH-IN-ALCOHOL STOUT THAT'S DARKER THAN A DANISH WINTER NIGHT.

//

MASH In a medium stockpot, heat 3 1/2 quarts (3.31 liters) water over high heat to 160°F (70°C). Add all the malts and stir gently. The temperature should reduce to 150°F (66°C) within 1 minute. Turn off the heat. Steep the grains for 60 minutes between 144°F and 152°F (62°C and 67°C). Every 10 minutes, stir and take the temperature. If the grains get too cold, turn the heat to high and stir until the temperature rises to that range, then turn off the heat. With 10 minutes left, in a second medium stockpot heat 1 gallon (3.79 liters) water to 170°F (77°C). After the grains have steeped for 60 minutes, turn the heat to high and stir until the temperature reaches 170°F (77°C). Turn off the heat.

SPARGE Place a fine-mesh strainer over a stock-pot and pour the grains into the strainer, reserving the liquid. Pour the 1 gallon (3.79 liters) of 170°F (77°C) water over the grains. Recirculate the collected liquid though the grains once.

BOIL Return the pot with the liquid to the stove and bring to a boil over high heat. When the liquid starts to foam, reduce the heat to a slow rolling boil and add the Magnum hops. After 45 minutes, add the Chinook hops. Add the Cascade and Styrian Golding hops after 89 minutes. Prepare an ice bath by stopping the sink and filling it halfway with water and ice. At the 90-minute mark, turn off the heat. Place the pot in the ice bath and cool to 70°F (21°C), about 30 minutes.

FERMENT Using a funnel and a strainer, pour the liquid into a sanitized fermenter. Add water as needed to fill the jug to the 1-gallon mark. Add the yeast, sanitize your hands, cover the mouth of the jug with one hand, and shake to distribute evenly. Attach a sanitized stopper and tubing to the fermenter and insert the other end of the tubing into a small bowl of sanitizing solution. The solution will begin to bubble as the yeast activates, pushing gas through the tube. Wait 2 to 3 days, until the bubbling has slowed, then replace the tubing system with an airlock. Wait 11 more days, then bottle, using the maple syrup (see page 13 for bottling instructions).

FERMENT

Belgian ale yeast, such as Safale S-33 (see note, page 16)

3 tablespoons (63 grams) maple syrup, for bottling

//

SUGGESTED FOOD PAIRINGS Maple glazed ham, stuffing, Christmas cookies

FOR 5 GALLONS

60-MINUTE MASH AT 152°F (67°C)

4 1/4 gallons (16.09 liters) of water, plus 4 gallons (15.14 liters) for sparging; 11.29 pounds (5121.06 grams) German Pilsner malt; 1.54 pounds (698.53 grams) Caramel 120 malt; 1.11 pounds (503.49 grams) Chocolate malt; 1.03 pounds (467.20 grams) Special B malt; 1.03 pounds (467.20 grams) Beechwood Smoked malt; 1.03 pounds (467.20 grams) roasted barley

90-MINUTE BOIL 0.81 ounces (22.96 grams) Magnum hops; 0.71 ounces (20.13 grams) Chinook hops; 1.42 ounces (40.26 grams) Cascade hops; 1.42 ounces (40.26 grams) Styrian Golding hops

FERMENT Belgian ale yeast, such as Safale S-33; 1 cup (340 grams) maple syrup, for bottling

BAMBERG ONION

MAKES 4

4 large white or Vidalia onions

4 slices bacon, diced

¼ lb (113.4 g) ground turkey

1 large egg

1 cup (0.24 l) panko

½ cup (0.12 l) chopped fresh flat-leaf parsley

Salt and pepper to taste

1 cup (0.24 l) Smoked Wheat (page 142) or other smoked beer

WE'VE LIGHTENED UP THE TRADITIONALLY PORK-STUFFED BAMBERG MAINSTAY JUST A TOUCH BY ADDING GROUND TURKEY AND A FISTFUL OF FRESH HERBS. THE RESULT STAYS TRUE TO THE SPIRIT OF THE DISH MADE FAMOUS BY THE QUAINT, BEER-LOVING TOWN THAT SCHLENKERLA (SEE PAGE 140) CALLS HOME.

//

1 Preheat the oven to 375°F (191°C).

2 Peel the onions and cut off the top and bottom so the onions can sit upright. From the top end, hollow out the insides with a spoon, reserving the insides, until the sides are about ¼ inch (0.64 centimeter) thick. Set the onion shells aside.

3 Dice the inside of the onions. Place the bacon in a sauté pan over medium-high heat. A minute later add the onion and cook with the bacon until soft, about 5 minutes. Drain off all but 1 tablespoon of the rendered fat. Let the mixture cool.

4 In a mixing bowl, combine the cooked onion and bacon with the ground turkey, egg, panko, and parsley. Season with salt and pepper.

5 Fill the onion shells with the mixture, set them upright in a baking dish, and pour in the beer. Roast, uncovered, for about 45 minutes, until the onions are tender and the filling is cooked through.

6 Transfer the onions to a serving dish and drizzle with the pan drippings.

WELSH RAREBIT BEER FONDUE

SERVES 4

1 cup (0.24 l) Smoked Wheat (page 142) or other dark roasted or smoked beer

10.5 oz (0.31 l) condensed tomato soup

1 tsp (5 g) Dijon mustard

1 tsp (5.73 g) Worcestershire sauce

1 tsp (5.73 g) hot sauce

12 oz (340.2 g) cheddar cheese, shredded

½ cup (0.12 l) heavy cream

Peasant bread loaf, cubed and toasted

WELSH RAREBIT TRADITIONALLY IS TOAST TOPPED WITH A CHEDDAR AND ALE SAUCE. ERICA GREW UP WITH A BASTARDIZED FONDUE VERSION HER MOM MADE THAT CALLED FOR A CAN OF TOMATO SOUP, A CUP OF MILK, AND A WHOLE LOT OF AMERICAN CHEESE. WHEN WE CAME ACROSS THE PROPER BEER-FUELED PUB VERSION, ERICA WENT FROM FEELING ECSTATIC (CHILDHOOD FAVORITE + BEER!) TO A BIT CONFUSED (WAIT, *THAT'S* HOW IT'S SPELLED?), TO FINALLY BEING SLIGHTLY DISAPPOINTED UPON TASTING THE DISH (TOAST AND STRINGY BEER CHEESE). SO WE GOT TO WORK CREATING A VERSION THAT COMBINED HER FAVORITE ASPECTS OF BOTH: IN WENT THE BEER, WORCESTERSHIRE SAUCE, AND CHEDDAR, BUT THE TOMATO SOUP, CREAM, AND FONDUE APPROACH STAYED AS WELL.

1 In a saucepan over medium-high heat, combine the beer, tomato soup, mustard, Worcestershire, and hot sauce. Whisk until well blended.

2 When the mixture starts to simmer, add the cheddar a handful at a time and whisk until it completely melts. Remove from the heat and whisk in the cream. Serve fondue style with skewers of cubed bread.

BEER-SOAKED OVEN FRIES

SERVES 6 TO 8

4 lb (1814.37 g) russet potatoes, cut into wedges

3 cups (0.71 l) light, flavorful beer such as Bruxelles Blonde (page 102)

3 Tbsp (39 g) olive oil

½ tsp (2 g) coarse salt

Salt and pepper

THE ACT OF FRYING SOMETHING IS OFTEN A DANCE AROUND THE STOVE, ARM AND TONG OUTSTRETCHED TO AVOID THE POP OF OIL THAT COMES WHEN WHATEVER YOU ARE FRYING IS NOT QUITE AS DRY AS YOU THOUGHT. WHICH IS WHY THE IDEA OF SOMETHING BEING BOTH SOAKED AND FRIED SOUNDS LIKE A BIT OF A DISASTER.

BUT SAFE IN THE OVEN, A WELL-SOAKED (IN OUR CASE, BEER-SOAKED) POTATO PUFFS UP FLUFFY IN THE MIDDLE WITH A CRISP GOLDEN EXTERIOR. WE FIND THESE UTTERLY ADDICTIVE ON THEIR OWN, BUT WHEN WE ARE CRAVING A NO-HOLDS-BARRED FRY FEST, WE GO FULL POUTINE STYLE (SEE BLACK PEPPER BEER POUTINE, PAGE 171).

1 Preheat the oven to 425°F (218°C).

2 Put the potatoes in a large bowl, cover with the beer, and let soak for 20 minutes. Drain the potatoes and pat dry with paper towels.

3 Toss the potatoes with the oil and coarse salt and spread them on a baking sheet in a single layer, being careful not to crowd them. Bake for 45 minutes (flipping halfway through) or until the outside is golden and crisp but not burnt.

4 Season with salt and pepper to taste. Serve hot.

BLACK PEPPER BEER POUTINE

SERVES 6 TO 8 AS AN INDULGENT MIDNIGHT SNACK

4 Tbsp (56 g) unsalted butter

¼ cup (32 g) all-purpose flour

2 shallots, minced

2 garlic cloves, minced

2 cups (0.47 l) beef stock

2 cups (0.47 l) dark beer

3 Tbsp (18.75 g) coarsely cracked black peppercorns

Salt

Beer-Soaked Oven Fries (page 170)

2 cups (260 g) cheddar cheese curds (see Sources, page 173)

IF YOU HAVE NOT HAD THE GRAVY-SOAKED, CHEESE CURD–TOPPED, FRENCH FRY CALORIE BOMB AND MONTREAL STAPLE CALLED POUTINE, YOU HAVE NOT LIVED. OR MORE ACCURATELY, YOU HAVE LIVED FAR HEALTHIER THAN US. OUR AGGRESSIVELY PEPPERED, BEER-SATURATED VERSION IS JAMMED WITH BEECHER'S CHEESE CURDS (FROM THE MANHATTAN OUTPOST OF SEATTLE'S LEGENDARY PIKE'S PLACE CHEESE SHOP) AND IS A LATE-NIGHT, POST-BEER-FEST FAVORITE.

1   Melt the butter in a saucepan over medium-high heat. Add the flour and whisk until smooth. Add the shallot and garlic and cook, stirring, until soft, about 2 minutes. Add the stock, beer, and peppercorns and bring to a boil, stirring constantly, until thickened, about 6 minutes. Remove from the heat. Add salt to taste.

2   Pour the gravy over the fries and top with cheese curds. Devour immediately.

PLANNING YOUR BREW TRIP

One of our favorite things about beer is that it is incredibly local. Small production facilities and weird state-by-state liquor and distribution laws means that a lot of beer never leaves its state (or even city in some cases), so you have to go to it. On our trips, we seek out breweries we've heard great things about or were lucky enough to try at a festival. But we also stumble upon local options that make our day. Whether you're just looking for an evening escape at a work conference, tacking on extra days for a friend's cross-country wedding, or planning a full-fledged beer trip, these tips will get your brew trip, no matter what length, heading In the right direction.

1 FIND THE BEER

Find the breweries, brewpubs, and craft beer bars a particular city or region has to offer on a website like beeradvocate.com, ratebeer.com, or craftbeer.com.

2 MAP IT OUT

Breweries need space, space that they can afford, and space that is zoned accordingly—which means production breweries are often on the outskirts and industrial parts of town. Brewpubs and craft beer bars are more likely to be in easily accessible places. Map out the public transit options or get the numbers of local cab companies.

3 LOOK FOR BEER EVENTS & FESTIVALS

Use the same websites mentioned above together with local newspapers, magazines, and blogs to get a sense of what might be happening during your visit. Beer festivals are an amazing way to try beers from way more breweries than you could at a bar. A good festival can leave you with the taste of a whole region. Plus, you often get a chance to meet the very brewer who made the beers you're drinking.

4 CHECK IN WITH THE BREWERY

Brewery websites and social media feeds are the best places for up-to-the-minute information on beer dinners, brewer's nights at local bars, what's just been tapped in the tasting room, or alerts if breweries have changed their hours. Many breweries host tours (be prepared to wear goggles and closed-toe shoes), but you may need to sign up for some of the most popular ones in advance. Email smaller breweries that don't have tours ahead of time. Tell them that you really love their beers, and ask where to find the best place to enjoy them locally—they may have tasting hours you didn't know about, or they may recommend a local bar or restaurant that serves specialties of the region.

5 GO TO A BEER CITY

Whether it's the water, proximity to hop farms, or history, some places just seem to breed breweries. And we love them for it. A few of our favorites are Asheville, North Carolina; Boulder, Colorado; Portland, Oregon; St. Louis, Missouri; Chicago, Illinois; Bamberg, Germany; any city in Belgium; Twin Cities, Minnesota; and Austin, Texas—and of course the beer city where we live, work, brew, and drink: Brooklyn, New York.

6 BE FRIENDLY

Chat with the bartenders and folks drinking the beer alongside you. We have had plenty of friendly bartenders give us impromptu tours, tip us off that they have started barrel aging a certain beer, or list restaurants we should not miss. In a tasting room setting at smaller breweries, the person serving your beer often has had a hand in making it (even if it was just washing kegs or being a human conveyor belt). The same goes for your fellow beer drinkers—if they are sitting alone, scribbling notes, or just as chatty with the bartender as you are, they are likely fellow beer travelers and might have some great tips for other places in town.

7 NARROW IT DOWN

There is a lot of beer out there. Choose the beers and breweries you are most excited about and stick with those (and those nearby). Otherwise you will have quite a bit of explaining to do when people ask if you saw the Alamo, Big Ben, or the Empire State Building. Don't miss all the sights in a city in your attempt to drink all the beer.

8 SAMPLERS ARE YOUR BEST FRIEND

We love beer flights, and prefer the diversity of three tasting-size pours to a pint. But not every brewery or bar offers flights (and even those that do likely don't offer them during peak hours). Look on their websites ahead of time for information. Traveling with a beer-loving friend who doesn't mind sharing glasses with you is very helpful. Water, regular meals, and workouts are advisable, too.

9 TAKE NOTES

We do two o'clock tastings with our staff a few times a week where we taste and take notes on different beers. We always joke that a bar isn't the best place to retain information on a beer. And it's true. If you try something at a brewery that you haven't heard of before, write it down. Brewery tasting rooms are the best place to get one-off and limited-release batches that don't make it into bottles and they won't necessarily be listed on the brewery website. Writing it down may inspire your next batch.

10 SAY THANKS

Brewing is hard work. The reward for lifting sacks of grain all day shouldn't just be increased upper body strength. If you like a beer, let the brewer know. Most great brewers make beer that they like to drink, and letting them know you appreciate what they're doing says keep up the good, wet, heavy-lifting, often-tedious, backbreakingly hard work.

SOURCES

BREW SUPPLY STORES

BROOKLYN BREW SHOP

www.brooklynbrewshop.com
info@brooklynbrewshop.com
FOR: 1 gallon kits, equipment, ingredient mixes

Brooklyn Brew Shop ingredient mixes and kits are also available at Whole Foods Markets, Williams-Sonoma, and specialty stores nationwide. For a full list of retailers see: brooklynbrewshop.com/locator.

HOME BREWERS ASSOCIATION

www.homebrewersassociation.org
FOR: Local brew supply shop listings

MORE BEER!

www.morebeer.com
FOR: General Brewing Equipment, Brewing Ingredients

KALUSTYANS

www.kalustyans.com
FOR: Spices, Teas, and specialty foods

SPICE STATION

www.spicestationsilverlake.com
FOR: Spices

STUMPTOWN COFFEE

www.stumptowncoffee.com
FOR: Coffee

WHOLE FOODS MARKETS

Multiple locations
www.wholefoodsmarket.com
FOR: Spices, gluten-free grains, specialty foods

LOCAL PRODUCE

GROW NYC

www.grownyc.org
FOR: New York City farmer's markets

LOCAL HARVEST

www.localharvest.org
FOR: U.S. farmer's markets

ACKNOWLEDGMENTS

To all the brewers and breweries (both those who are featured in this book and those we just joined for an afternoon) for opening up their doors and bottles for us. Especially:

The Bruery's Benjamin Weiss; Jester King's Jeffrey Stuffings and Ron Extract; Upright Brewing's Alex Ganum and tasting room Brent; Goose Island's Ken Hunnemeder and Mark Kamarauskas; Ranger Creek's Rob Landerman and Mark McDavid; Fullsteam's Sean Lilly Wilson and Chris Davis; Cigar City's Justin Clark, Joseph J M Redner, Toni Derby and Geiger Powell; Pretty Thing's Martha Holley-Paquette, Dann Paquette, and beer historian Ron Pattinson; Evil Twin's Jeppe Jarnit-Bjergsø; Dieu de Ciel's Jean-Francois Gravel; Hopenstark's Fred Cormier; The Alchemist's Jen and John Kimmich and cellarman Steve Miller; Jenlain's Raymond Duyck and Audrey Saint-Leger; Vanberg and Dewulf's Wendy Littlefield; Dilewyn's Anne-Catherine and Vincent Dilewyn; The Kernel's Evin O'Riordain; B United's Matthias Neidhart; Hill Farmstead's Shaun E Hill; Pausa Cafe's Andrea Bertola, Gabriele Genduso and Stefano; Brooklyn Brewery's Steve Hindy, Garrett Oliver and Glenn Severance; Carton Brewing's Augie Carton; Logsdon's Dave Logsdon and Charles Porter; Bunker Brewing's Chresten Sorensen and Jay Villani; Wicked Weed's Walt and Luke Dickinson; Pisgah Brewing's Jeremy Austin and Benton Wharton; Odell Brewing's Brendan McGivney and Doug Odell.

To Birrificio Montegioco's Riccardo Franzosi and crew for the most magical of afternoons. And to Schlenkerla's Matthais Trum for letting us throw a log onto the fire.

To Deryck Vonn Lee, who has been designing for us from day zero and did the wonderful illustrations for both our books.

To Bob Mecoy, our beer-brewing super agent.

To Angelin Borsics, Emily Takoudes, Pam Krauss, and everyone at Clarkson Potter for helping us share our passion with the world.

To our growing Brooklyn-based staff. And our customers now worldwide (we hope you enjoy the metric).

To our friends who listen to us talk endlessly about beer and to those who hosted us during our travels: Erin and Adam Lane, Carson and Alison Werner, Amanda and Larry McMahon, Molly Freiberg, Jordan Saia, and the many couchsurfing hosts who somehow let us sleep in their homes.

To our families. And to each other.

INDEX